Licensing Act 2003

CHAPTER 17

Explanatory Notes are available separately

GRAN*GIS* UK Publishing

Adapted and published by GRANGIS (Grand Register Library).
Online: www.grangis.com
E-mail: contact@grangis.com

In this version:
ISBN: 979-8-88559-025-9

Note: This is the original version (as it was originally enacted). Title, sub-title and the generated date is as marked on the pages.

Licensing Act 2003

CHAPTER 17

LICENSING ACT 2003

PART 1

LICENSABLE ACTIVITIES

PART 2

LICENSING AUTHORITIES

The authorities

Functions of licensing authorities etc.

Licensing committees

PART 3

PREMISES LICENCES

Introductory

Grant of premises licence

Duration of licence

Provisional statement

Duty to notify certain changes

Variation of licences

Transfer of premises licence

Licensing Act 2003

2003 CHAPTER 17

An Act to make provision about the regulation of the sale and supply of alcohol, the provision of entertainment and the provision of late night refreshment, about offences relating to alcohol and for connected purposes. [10th July 2003]

BE IT ENACTED by the Queen's most Excellent Majesty, by and with the advice and consent of the Lords Spiritual and Temporal, and Commons, in this present Parliament assembled, and by the authority of the same, as follows:—

PART 1

LICENSABLE ACTIVITIES

1 Licensable activities and qualifying club activities

(1) For the purposes of this Act the following are licensable activities—

(a) the sale by retail of alcohol,

(b) the supply of alcohol by or on behalf of a club to, or to the order of, a member of the club,

(c) the provision of regulated entertainment, and

(d) the provision of late night refreshment.

(2) For those purposes the following licensable activities are also qualifying club activities—

(a) the supply of alcohol by or on behalf of a club to, or to the order of, a member of the club,

(b) the sale by retail of alcohol by or on behalf of a club to a guest of a member of the club for consumption on the premises where the sale takes place, and

(c) the provision of regulated entertainment where that provision is by or on behalf of a club for members of the club or members of the club and their guests.

(3) In this Act references to the supply of alcohol by or on behalf of a club to, or to the order of, a member of the club do not include a reference to any supply which is a sale by retail of alcohol.

(4) Schedule 1 makes provision about what constitutes the provision of regulated entertainment for the purposes of this Act.

(5) Schedule 2 makes provision about what constitutes the provision of late night refreshment for those purposes (including provision that certain activities carried on in relation to certain clubs or hotels etc, or certain employees, do not constitute provision of late night refreshment and are, accordingly, not licensable activities).

(6) For the purposes of this Act premises are "used" for a licensable activity if that activity is carried on on or from the premises.

(7) This section is subject to sections 173 to 175 (which exclude activities from the definition of licensable activity in certain circumstances).

2 Authorisation for licensable activities and qualifying club activities

(1) A licensable activity may be carried on—

(a) under and in accordance with a premises licence (see Part 3), or

(b) in circumstances where the activity is a permitted temporary activity by virtue of Part 5.

(2) A qualifying club activity may be carried on under and in accordance with a club premises certificate (see Part 4).

(3) Nothing in this Act prevents two or more authorisations having effect concurrently in respect of the whole or a part of the same premises or in respect of the same person.

(4) For the purposes of subsection (3) "authorisation" means—

(a) a premises licence;

(b) a club premises certificate;

(c) a temporary event notice.

PART 2

LICENSING AUTHORITIES

The authorities

3 Licensing authorities

(1) In this Act "licensing authority" means—

(a) the council of a district in England,

(b) the council of a county in England in which there are no district councils,

(c) the council of a county or county borough in Wales,

(d) the council of a London borough,

(e) the Common Council of the City of London,

(f) the Sub-Treasurer of the Inner Temple,

(g) the Under-Treasurer of the Middle Temple, or
(h) the Council of the Isles of Scilly.

(2) For the purposes of this Act, a licensing authority's area is the area for which the authority acts.

Functions of licensing authorities etc.

4 General duties of licensing authorities

(1) A licensing authority must carry out its functions under this Act ("licensing functions") with a view to promoting the licensing objectives.

(2) The licensing objectives are—
(a) the prevention of crime and disorder;
(b) public safety;
(c) the prevention of public nuisance; and
(d) the protection of children from harm.

(3) In carrying out its licensing functions, a licensing authority must also have regard to—
(a) its licensing statement published under section 5, and
(b) any guidance issued by the Secretary of State under section 182.

5 Statement of licensing policy

(1) Each licensing authority must in respect of each three year period—
(a) determine its policy with respect to the exercise of its licensing functions, and
(b) publish a statement of that policy (a "licensing statement") before the beginning of the period.

(2) In this section "three year period" means—
(a) the period of three years beginning with such day as the Secretary of State may by order appoint, and
(b) each subsequent period of three years.

(3) Before determining its policy for a three year period, a licensing authority must consult—
(a) the chief officer of police for the licensing authority's area,
(b) the fire authority for that area,
(c) such persons as the licensing authority considers to be representative of holders of premises licences issued by that authority,
(d) such persons as the licensing authority considers to be representative of holders of club premises certificates issued by that authority,
(e) such persons as the licensing authority considers to be representative of holders of personal licences issued by that authority, and
(f) such other persons as the licensing authority considers to be representative of businesses and residents in its area.

(4) During each three year period, a licensing authority must keep its policy under review and make such revisions to it, at such times, as it considers appropriate.

(5) Subsection (3) applies in relation to any revision of an authority's policy as it applies in relation to the original determination of that policy.

(6) Where revisions are made, the licensing authority must publish a statement of the revisions or the revised licensing statement.

(7) Regulations may make provision about the determination and revision of policies, and the preparation and publication of licensing statements, under this section.

6 Licensing committees

(1) Each licensing authority must establish a licensing committee consisting of at least ten, but not more than fifteen, members of the authority.

(2) This section does not apply in relation to the Sub-Treasurer of the Inner Temple or the Under-Treasurer of the Middle Temple.

7 Exercise and delegation of functions

(1) All matters relating to the discharge by a licensing authority of its licensing functions are, by virtue of this subsection, referred to its licensing committee and, accordingly, that committee must discharge those functions on behalf of the authority.

(2) Subsection (1) does not apply to—

(a) any function conferred on the licensing authority by section 5 (statement of licensing policy), or

(b) any function discharged under subsection (5)(a) below by a committee (other than a licensing committee),

or any matter relating to the discharge of any such function.

(3) A licensing authority may arrange for the discharge by its licensing committee of any function of the authority which—

(a) relates to a matter referred to that committee by virtue of subsection (1), but

(b) is not a licensing function.

(4) Where the licensing authority does not make arrangements under subsection (3) in respect of any such function, it must (unless the matter is urgent) consider a report of its licensing committee with respect to the matter before discharging the function.

(5) Where a matter relates to a licensing function of a licensing authority and to a function of the authority which is not a licensing function ("the other function"), the authority may—

(a) refer the matter to another of its committees and arrange for the discharge of the licensing function by that committee, or

(b) refer the matter to its licensing committee (to the extent it is not already so referred under subsection (1)) and arrange for the discharge of the other function by the licensing committee.

(6) In a case where an authority exercises its power under subsection (5)(a), the committee to which the matter is referred must (unless the matter is urgent) consider a report of the authority's licensing committee with respect to the matter before discharging the function concerned.

(7) Before exercising its power under subsection (5)(b), an authority must consult its licensing committee.

(8) In a case where an authority exercises its power under subsection (5)(b), its licensing committee must (unless the matter is urgent) consider any report of any of the authority's other committees with respect to the matter before discharging the function concerned.

(9) Where a licensing committee is unable to discharge any function delegated to it in accordance with this section because of the number of its members who are unable to take part in the consideration or discussion of any matter or vote on any question with respect to it, the committee must refer the matter back to the licensing authority and the authority must discharge that function.

(10) This section does not apply in relation to the Sub-Treasurer of the Inner Temple or the Under-Treasurer of the Middle Temple.

8 Requirement to keep a register

(1) Each licensing authority must keep a register containing—

(a) a record of each premises licence, club premises certificate and personal licence issued by it,

(b) a record of each temporary event notice received by it,

(c) the matters mentioned in Schedule 3, and

(d) such other information as may be prescribed.

(2) Regulations may require a register kept under this section to be in a prescribed form and kept in a prescribed manner.

(3) Each licensing authority must provide facilities for making the information contained in the entries in its register available for inspection (in a legible form) by any person during office hours and without payment.

(4) If requested to do so by any person, a licensing authority must supply him with a copy of the information contained in any entry in its register in legible form.

(5) A licensing authority may charge such reasonable fee as it may determine in respect of any copy supplied under subsection (4).

(6) The Secretary of State may arrange for the duties conferred on licensing authorities by this section to be discharged by means of one or more central registers kept by a person appointed pursuant to the arrangements.

(7) The Secretary of State may require licensing authorities to participate in and contribute towards the cost of any arrangements made under subsection (6).

Licensing committees

9 Proceedings of licensing committee

(1) A licensing committee may establish one or more sub-committees consisting of three members of the committee.

(2) Regulations may make provision about—

(a) the proceedings of licensing committees and their sub-committees (including provision about the validity of proceedings and the quorum for meetings),

(b) public access to the meetings of those committees and sub-committees,

(c) the publicity to be given to those meetings,

(d) the agendas and records to be produced in respect of those meetings, and

(e) public access to such agendas and records and other information about those meetings.

(3) Subject to any such regulations, each licensing committee may regulate its own procedure and that of its sub-committees.

10 Sub-delegation of functions by licensing committee etc.

(1) A licensing committee may arrange for the discharge of any functions exercisable by it—

(a) by a sub-committee established by it, or

(b) subject to subsection (4), by an officer of the licensing authority.

(2) Where arrangements are made under subsection (1)(a), then, subject to subsections (4) and (5), the sub-committee may in turn arrange for the discharge of the function concerned by an officer of the licensing authority.

(3) Arrangements under subsection (1) or (2) may provide for more than one sub-committee or officer to discharge the same function concurrently.

(4) Arrangements may not be made under subsection (1) or (2) for the discharge by an officer of—

(a) any function under—

(i) section 18(3) (determination of application for premises licence where representations have been made),

(ii) section 31(3) (determination of application for provisional statement where representations have been made),

(iii) section 35(3) (determination of application for variation of premises licence where representations have been made),

(iv) section 39(3) (determination of application to vary designated premises supervisor following police objection),

(v) section 44(5) (determination of application for transfer of premises licence following police objection),

(vi) section 48(3) (consideration of police objection made to interim authority notice),

(vii) section 72(3) (determination of application for club premises certificate where representations have been made),

(viii) section 85(3)(determination of application to vary club premises certificate where representations have been made),

(ix) section 105(2) (decision to give counter notice following police objection to temporary event notice),

(x) section 120(7) (determination of application for grant of personal licence following police objection),

(xi) section 121(6) (determination of application for renewal of personal licence following police objection), or

(xii) section 124(4) (revocation of licence where convictions come to light after grant etc.),

(b) any function under section 52(2) or (3) (determination of application for review of premises licence) in a case where relevant representations (within the meaning of section 52(7)) have been made,

(c) any function under section 88(2) or (3) (determination of application for review of club premises certificate) in a case where relevant representations (within the meaning of section 88(7)) have been made, or

(d) any function under section 167(5) (review following closure order), in a case where relevant representations (within the meaning of section 167(9)) have been made.

(5) The power exercisable under subsection (2) by a sub-committee established by a licensing committee is also subject to any direction given by that committee to the sub-committee.

PART 3

PREMISES LICENCES

Introductory

11 Premises licence

In this Act "premises licence" means a licence granted under this Part, in respect of any premises, which authorises the premises to be used for one or more licensable activities.

12 The relevant licensing authority

(1) For the purposes of this Part the "relevant licensing authority" in relation to any premises is determined in accordance with this section.

(2) Subject to subsection (3), the relevant licensing authority is the authority in whose area the premises are situated.

(3) Where the premises are situated in the areas of two or more licensing authorities, the relevant licensing authority is—

(a) the licensing authority in whose area the greater or greatest part of the premises is situated, or

(b) if there is no authority to which paragraph (a) applies, such one of those authorities as is nominated in accordance with subsection (4).

(4) In a case within subsection (3)(b)—

(a) an applicant for a premises licence must nominate one of the licensing authorities as the relevant licensing authority in relation to the application and any licence granted as a result of it, and

(b) an applicant for a statement under section 29 (provisional statement) in respect of the premises must nominate one of the licensing authorities as the relevant licensing authority in relation to the statement.

13 Authorised persons, interested parties and responsible authorities

(1) In this Part in relation to any premises each of the following expressions has the meaning given to it by this section—

"authorised person",

"interested party",

"responsible authority".

(2) "Authorised person" means any of the following—

(a) an officer of a licensing authority in whose area the premises are situated who is authorised by that authority for the purposes of this Act,

(b) an inspector appointed under section 18 of the Fire Precautions Act 1971 (c. 40),

(c) an inspector appointed under section 19 of the Health and Safety at Work etc. Act 1974 (c. 37),

(d) an officer of a local authority, in whose area the premises are situated, who is authorised by that authority for the purposes of exercising one or more of its statutory functions in relation to minimising or preventing the risk of pollution of the environment or of harm to human health,

(e) in relation to a vessel, an inspector, or a surveyor of ships, appointed under section 256 of the Merchant Shipping Act 1995 (c. 21),

(f) a person prescribed for the purposes of this subsection.

(3) "Interested party" means any of the following—

(a) a person living in the vicinity of the premises,

(b) a body representing persons who live in that vicinity,

(c) a person involved in a business in that vicinity,

(d) a body representing persons involved in such businesses.

(4) "Responsible authority" means any of the following—

(a) the chief officer of police for any police area in which the premises are situated,

(b) the fire authority for any area in which the premises are situated,

(c) the enforcing authority within the meaning given by section 18 of the Health and Safety at Work etc. Act 1974 for any area in which the premises are situated,

(d) the local planning authority within the meaning given by the Town and Country Planning Act 1990 (c. 8) for any area in which the premises are situated,

(e) the local authority by which statutory functions are exercisable in any area in which the premises are situated in relation to minimising or preventing the risk of pollution of the environment or of harm to human health,

(f) a body which—

(i) represents those who, in relation to any such area, are responsible for, or interested in, matters relating to the protection of children from harm, and

(ii) is recognised by the licensing authority for that area for the purposes of this section as being competent to advise it on such matters,

(g) any licensing authority (other than the relevant licensing authority) in whose area part of the premises is situated,

(h) in relation to a vessel—
  (i) a navigation authority (within the meaning of section 221(1) of the Water Resources Act 1991 (c. 57) having functions in relation to the waters where the vessel is usually moored or berthed or any waters where it is, or is proposed to be, navigated at a time when it is used for licensable activities,
  (ii) the Environment Agency,
  (iii) the British Waterways Board, or
  (iv) the Secretary of State,
(i) a person prescribed for the purposes of this subsection.

(5) For the purposes of this section, "statutory function" means a function conferred by or under any enactment.

14 Meaning of "supply of alcohol"

For the purposes of this Part the "supply of alcohol" means—
(a) the sale by retail of alcohol, or
(b) the supply of alcohol by or on behalf of a club to, or to the order of, a member of the club.

15 Meaning of "designated premises supervisor"

(1) In this Act references to the "designated premises supervisor", in relation to a premises licence, are to the individual for the time being specified in that licence as the premises supervisor.

(2) Nothing in this Act prevents an individual who holds a premises licence from also being specified in the licence as the premises supervisor.

Grant of premises licence

16 Applicant for premises licence

(1) The following persons may apply for a premises licence—
(a) a person who carries on, or proposes to carry on, a business which involves the use of the premises for the licensable activities to which the application relates,
(b) a person who makes the application pursuant to—
  (i) any statutory function discharged by that person which relates to those licensable activities, or
  (ii) any function discharged by that person by virtue of Her Majesty's prerogative,
(c) a recognised club,
(d) a charity,
(e) the proprietor of an educational institution,
(f) a health service body,
(g) a person who is registered under Part 2 of the Care Standards Act 2000 (c. 14) in respect of an independent hospital,

(h) the chief officer of police of a police force in England and Wales,

(i) a person of such other description as may be prescribed.

(2) But an individual may not apply for a premises licence unless he is aged 18 or over.

(3) In this section—

"charity" has the same meaning as in section 96(1) of the Charities Act 1993 (c. 10);

"educational institution" means—

(a) a school, or an institution within the further or higher education sector, within the meaning of section 4 of the Education Act 1996 (c. 56), or

(b) a college (including any institution in the nature of a college), school, hall or other institution of a university, in circumstances where the university receives financial support under section 65 of the Further and Higher Education Act 1992 (c. 13);

"health service body" means—

(a) an NHS trust established by virtue of section 5 of the National Health Service and Community Care Act 1990 (c. 19),

(b) a Primary Care Trust established by virtue of section 16A of the National Health Service Act 1977 (c. 49), or

(c) a Local Health Board established by virtue of section 16BA of that Act;

"independent hospital" has the same meaning as in section 2(2) of the Care Standards Act 2000 (c. 14);

"proprietor"—

(a) in relation to a school within the meaning of section 4 of the Education Act 1996, has the same meaning as in section 579(1) of that Act, and

(b) in relation to an educational institution other than such a school, means the governing body of that institution within the meaning of section 90(1) of the Further and Higher Education Act 1992; and

"statutory function" means a function conferred by or under any enactment.

17 Application for premises licence

(1) An application for a premises licence must be made to the relevant licensing authority.

(2) Subsection (1) is subject to regulations under—

(a) section 54 (form etc. of applications etc.);

(b) section 55 (fees to accompany applications etc.).

(3) An application under this section must also be accompanied—

(a) by an operating schedule,

(b) by a plan of the premises to which the application relates, in the prescribed form, and

(c) if the licensable activities to which the application relates ("the relevant licensable activities") include the supply of alcohol, by a form of consent in the prescribed form given by the individual whom the applicant wishes to have specified in the premises licence as the premises supervisor.

(4) An "operating schedule" is a document which is in the prescribed form and includes a statement of the following matters—

(a) the relevant licensable activities,

(b) the times during which it is proposed that the relevant licensable activities are to take place,

(c) any other times during which it is proposed that the premises are to be open to the public,

(d) where the applicant wishes the licence to have effect for a limited period, that period,

(e) where the relevant licensable activities include the supply of alcohol, prescribed information in respect of the individual whom the applicant wishes to have specified in the premises licence as the premises supervisor,

(f) where the relevant licensable activities include the supply of alcohol, whether the supplies are proposed to be for consumption on the premises or off the premises, or both,

(g) the steps which it is proposed to take to promote the licensing objectives,

(h) such other matters as may be prescribed.

(5) The Secretary of State must by regulations—

(a) require an applicant to advertise his application within the prescribed period—

(i) in the prescribed form, and

(ii) in a manner which is prescribed and is likely to bring the application to the attention of the interested parties likely to be affected by it;

(b) require an applicant to give notice of his application to each responsible authority, and such other persons as may be prescribed, within the prescribed period;

(c) prescribe the period during which interested parties and responsible authorities may make representations to the relevant licensing authority about the application.

18 Determination of application for premises licence

(1) This section applies where the relevant licensing authority—

(a) receives an application for a premises licence made in accordance with section 17, and

(b) is satisfied that the applicant has complied with any requirement imposed on him under subsection (5) of that section.

(2) Subject to subsection (3), the authority must grant the licence in accordance with the application subject only to—

(a) such conditions as are consistent with the operating schedule accompanying the application, and

(b) any conditions which must under section 19, 20 or 21 be included in the licence.

(3) Where relevant representations are made, the authority must—

(a) hold a hearing to consider them, unless the authority, the applicant and each person who has made such representations agree that a hearing is unnecessary, and

(b) having regard to the representations, take such of the steps mentioned in subsection (4) (if any) as it considers necessary for the promotion of the licensing objectives.

(4) The steps are—

(a) to grant the licence subject to—
   (i) the conditions mentioned in subsection (2)(a) modified to such extent as the authority considers necessary for the promotion of the licensing objectives, and
   (ii) any condition which must under section 19, 20 or 21 be included in the licence;
(b) to exclude from the scope of the licence any of the licensable activities to which the application relates;
(c) to refuse to specify a person in the licence as the premises supervisor;
(d) to reject the application.

(5) For the purposes of subsection (4)(a)(i) the conditions mentioned in subsection (2)(a) are modified if any of them is altered or omitted or any new condition is added.

(6) For the purposes of this section, "relevant representations" means representations which—
(a) are about the likely effect of the grant of the premises licence on the promotion of the licensing objectives,
(b) meet the requirements of subsection (7),
(c) if they relate to the identity of the person named in the application as the proposed premises supervisor, meet the requirements of subsection (9), and
(d) are not excluded representations by virtue of section 32 (restriction on making representations following issue of provisional statement).

(7) The requirements of this subsection are—
(a) that the representations were made by an interested party or responsible authority within the period prescribed under section 17(5)(c),
(b) that they have not been withdrawn, and
(c) in the case of representations made by an interested party (who is not also a responsible authority), that they are not, in the opinion of the relevant licensing authority, frivolous or vexatious.

(8) Where the authority determines for the purposes of subsection (7)(c) that any representations are frivolous or vexatious, it must notify the person who made them of the reasons for its determination.

(9) The requirements of this subsection are that the representations—
(a) were made by a chief officer of police for a police area in which the premises are situated, and
(b) include a statement that, due to the exceptional circumstances of the case, he is satisfied that the designation of the person concerned as the premises supervisor under the premises licence would undermine the crime prevention objective.

(10) In discharging its duty under subsection (2) or (3)(b), a licensing authority may grant a licence under this section subject to different conditions in respect of—
(a) different parts of the premises concerned;
(b) different licensable activities.

19 Mandatory conditions where licence authorises supply of alcohol

(1) Where a premises licence authorises the supply of alcohol, the licence must include the following conditions.

(2) The first condition is that no supply of alcohol may be made under the premises licence—

(a) at a time when there is no designated premises supervisor in respect of the premises licence, or

(b) at a time when the designated premises supervisor does not hold a personal licence or his personal licence is suspended.

(3) The second condition is that every supply of alcohol under the premises licence must be made or authorised by a person who holds a personal licence.

20 Mandatory condition: exhibition of films

(1) Where a premises licence authorises the exhibition of films, the licence must include a condition requiring the admission of children to the exhibition of any film to be restricted in accordance with this section.

(2) Where the film classification body is specified in the licence, unless subsection (3)(b) applies, admission of children must be restricted in accordance with any recommendation made by that body.

(3) Where—

(a) the film classification body is not specified in the licence, or

(b) the relevant licensing authority has notified the holder of the licence that this subsection applies to the film in question,

admission of children must be restricted in accordance with any recommendation made by that licensing authority.

(4) In this section—

"children" means persons aged under 18; and

"film classification body" means the person or persons designated as the authority under section 4 of the Video Recordings Act 1984 (c. 39) (authority to determine suitability of video works for classification).

21 Mandatory condition: door supervision

(1) Where a premises licence includes a condition that at specified times one or more individuals must be at the premises to carry out a security activity, the licence must include a condition that each such individual must be licensed by the Security Industry Authority.

(2) But nothing in subsection (1) requires such a condition to be imposed—

(a) in respect of premises within paragraph 8(3)(a) of Schedule 2 to the Private Security Industry Act 2001 (c. 12) (premises with premises licences authorising plays or films), or

(b) in respect of premises in relation to—

(i) any occasion mentioned in paragraph 8(3)(b) or (c) of that Schedule (premises being used exclusively by club with club premises certificate, under a temporary event notice authorising plays or films or under a gaming licence), or

(ii) any occasion within paragraph 8(3)(d) of that Schedule (occasions prescribed by regulations under that Act).

(3) For the purposes of this section—

(a) "security activity" means an activity to which paragraph 2(1)(a) of that Schedule applies, and

(b) paragraph 8(5) of that Schedule (interpretation of references to an occasion) applies as it applies in relation to paragraph 8 of that Schedule.

22 Prohibited conditions: plays

(1) In relation to a premises licence which authorises the performance of plays, no condition may be attached to the licence as to the nature of the plays which may be performed, or the manner of performing plays, under the licence.

(2) But subsection (1) does not prevent a licensing authority imposing, in accordance with section 18(2)(a) or (3)(b), 35(3)(b) or 52(3), any condition which it considers necessary on the grounds of public safety.

23 Grant or rejection of application

(1) Where an application is granted under section 18, the relevant licensing authority must forthwith—

(a) give a notice to that effect to—

(i) the applicant,

(ii) any person who made relevant representations in respect of the application, and

(iii) the chief officer of police for the police area (or each police area) in which the premises are situated, and

(b) issue the applicant with the licence and a summary of it.

(2) Where relevant representations were made in respect of the application, the notice under subsection (1)(a) must state the authority's reasons for its decision as to the steps (if any) to take under section 18(3)(b).

(3) Where an application is rejected under section 18, the relevant licensing authority must forthwith give a notice to that effect, stating its reasons for the decision, to—

(a) the applicant,

(b) any person who made relevant representations in respect of the application, and

(c) the chief officer of police for the police area (or each police area) in which the premises are situated.

(4) In this section "relevant representations" has the meaning given in section 18(6).

24 Form of licence and summary

(1) A premises licence and the summary of a premises licence must be in the prescribed form.

(2) Regulations under subsection (1) must, in particular, provide for the licence to—
   (a) specify the name and address of the holder;
   (b) include a plan of the premises to which the licence relates;
   (c) if the licence has effect for a limited period, specify that period;
   (d) specify the licensable activities for which the premises may be used;
   (e) if the licensable activities include the supply of alcohol, specify the name and address of the individual (if any) who is the premises supervisor in respect of the licence;
   (f) specify the conditions subject to which the licence has effect.

25 Theft, loss, etc. of premises licence or summary

(1) Where a premises licence or summary is lost, stolen, damaged or destroyed, the holder of the licence may apply to the relevant licensing authority for a copy of the licence or summary.

(2) Subsection (1) is subject to regulations under section 55(1) (fee to accompany applications).

(3) Where an application is made in accordance with this section, the relevant licensing authority must issue the holder of the licence with a copy of the licence or summary (certified by the authority to be a true copy) if it is satisfied that—
   (a) the licence or summary has been lost, stolen, damaged or destroyed, and
   (b) where it has been lost or stolen, the holder has reported that loss or theft to the police.

(4) The copy issued under this section must be a copy of the premises licence or summary in the form in which it existed immediately before it was lost, stolen, damaged or destroyed.

(5) This Act applies in relation to a copy issued under this section as it applies in relation to an original licence or summary.

Duration of licence

26 Period of validity of premises licence

(1) Subject to sections 27 and 28, a premises licence has effect until such time as—
   (a) it is revoked under section 52, or
   (b) if it specifies that it has effect for a limited period, that period expires.

(2) But a premises licence does not have effect during any period when it is suspended under section 52.

27 Death, incapacity, insolvency etc. of licence holder

(1) A premises licence lapses if the holder of the licence—
   (a) dies,
   (b) becomes mentally incapable (within the meaning of section 13(1) of the Enduring Powers of Attorney Act 1985 (c. 29)),
   (c) becomes insolvent,

(d) is dissolved, or

(e) if it is a club, ceases to be a recognised club.

(2) This section is subject to sections 47 and 50 (which make provision for the reinstatement of the licence in certain circumstances).

(3) For the purposes of this section, an individual becomes insolvent on—

(a) the approval of a voluntary arrangement proposed by him,

(b) being adjudged bankrupt or having his estate sequestrated, or

(c) entering into a deed of arrangement made for the benefit of his creditors or a trust deed for his creditors.

(4) For the purposes of this section, a company becomes insolvent on—

(a) the approval of a voluntary arrangement proposed by its directors,

(b) the appointment of an administrator in respect of the company,

(c) the appointment of an administrative receiver in respect of the company, or

(d) going into liquidation.

(5) An expression used in this section and in the Insolvency Act 1986 (c. 45) has the same meaning in this section as in that Act.

28 Surrender of premises licence

(1) Where the holder of a premises licence wishes to surrender his licence he may give the relevant licensing authority a notice to that effect.

(2) The notice must be accompanied by the premises licence or, if that is not practicable, by a statement of the reasons for the failure to provide the licence.

(3) Where a notice of surrender is given in accordance with this section, the premises licence lapses on receipt of the notice by the authority.

(4) This section is subject to section 50 (which makes provision for the reinstatement in certain circumstances of a licence surrendered under this section).

Provisional statement

29 Application for a provisional statement where premises being built, etc.

(1) This section applies to premises which—

(a) are being or are about to be constructed for the purpose of being used for one or more licensable activities, or

(b) are being or are about to be extended or otherwise altered for that purpose (whether or not they are already being used for that purpose).

(2) A person may apply to the relevant licensing authority for a provisional statement if—

(a) he is interested in the premises, and

(b) where he is an individual, he is aged 18 or over.

(3) In this Act "provisional statement" means a statement issued under section 31(2) or (3)(c).

(4) Subsection (2) is subject to regulations under—

(a) section 54 (form etc. of applications etc.);
(b) section 55 (fees to accompany applications etc.).

(5) An application under this section must also be accompanied by a schedule of works.

(6) A schedule of works is a document in the prescribed form which includes—
(a) a statement made by or on behalf of the applicant including particulars of the premises to which the application relates and of the licensable activities for which the premises are to be used,
(b) plans of the work being or about to be done at the premises, and
(c) such other information as may be prescribed.

(7) For the purposes of this Part, in relation to any premises in respect of which an application for a provisional statement has been made, references to the work being satisfactorily completed are to work at the premises being completed in a manner which substantially complies with the schedule of works accompanying the application.

30 Advertisement of application for provisional statement

(1) This section applies where an application is made under section 29.

(2) The duty to make regulations imposed on the Secretary of State by section 17(5) (advertisement etc. of application) applies in relation to an application under section 29 as it applies in relation to an application under section 17.

(3) Regulations made under section 17(5)(a) by virtue of subsection (2) may, in particular, require advertisements to contain a statement in the prescribed form describing the effect of section 32 (restriction on representations following issue of a provisional statement).

31 Determination of application for provisional statement

(1) This section applies where the relevant licensing authority—
(a) receives a provisional statement application, and
(b) is satisfied that the applicant has complied with any requirement imposed on him by virtue of section 30.

(2) Where no relevant representations are made, the authority must issue the applicant with a statement to that effect.

(3) Where relevant representations are made, the authority must—
(a) hold a hearing to consider them, unless the authority, the applicant and each person who has made such representations agree that a hearing is unnecessary,
(b) determine whether, on the basis of those representations and the provisional statement application, it would consider it necessary to take any steps under section 18(3)(b) if, on the work being satisfactorily completed, it had to decide whether to grant a premises licence in the form described in the provisional statement application, and
(c) issue the applicant with a statement which—
(i) gives details of that determination, and
(ii) states the authority's reasons for its decision as to the steps (if any) that it would be necessary to take under section 18(3)(b).

(4) The licensing authority must give a copy of the provisional statement to—

(a) each person who made relevant representations, and

(b) the chief officer of police for each police area in which the premises are situated.

(5) In this section "relevant representations" means representations—

(a) which are about the likely effect on the licensing objectives of the grant of a premises licence in the form described in the provisional statement application, if the work at the premises was satisfactorily completed, and

(b) which meet the requirements of subsection (6).

(6) The requirements are—

(a) that the representations are made by an interested party or responsible authority within the period prescribed under section 17(5)(c) by virtue of section 30,

(b) that the representations have not been withdrawn, and

(c) in the case of representations made by an interested party (who is not also a responsible authority), that they are not, in the opinion of the relevant licensing authority, frivolous or vexatious.

(7) Where the authority determines for the purposes of subsection (6)(c) that any representations are frivolous or vexatious, it must notify the person who made them of the reasons for its determination.

(8) In this section "provisional statement application" means an application made in accordance with section 29.

32 Restriction on representations following provisional statement

(1) This section applies where a provisional statement has been issued in respect of any premises ("the relevant premises") and a person subsequently applies for a premises licence in respect of—

(a) the relevant premises or a part of them, or

(b) premises that are substantially the same as the relevant premises or a part of them.

(2) Where—

(a) the application for the premises licence is an application for a licence in the same form as the licence described in the application for the provisional statement, and

(b) the work described in the schedule of works accompanying the application for that statement has been satisfactorily completed,

representations made by a person ("the relevant person") in respect of the application for the premises licence are excluded representations for the purposes of section 18(6)(d) if subsection (3) applies.

(3) This subsection applies if—

(a) given the information provided in the application for the provisional statement, the relevant person could have made the same, or substantially the same, representations about that application but failed to do so, without reasonable excuse, and

(b) there has been no material change in circumstances relating either to the relevant premises or to the area in the vicinity of those premises since the provisional statement was made.

Duty to notify certain changes

33 Notification of change of name or address

(1) The holder of a premises licence must, as soon as is reasonably practicable, notify the relevant licensing authority of any change in—

(a) his name or address,

(b) unless the designated premises supervisor has already notified the authority under subsection (4), the name or address of that supervisor.

(2) Subsection (1) is subject to regulations under section 55(1) (fee to accompany application).

(3) A notice under subsection (1) must also be accompanied by the premises licence (or the appropriate part of the licence) or, if that is not practicable, by a statement of the reasons for the failure to produce the licence (or part).

(4) Where the designated premises supervisor under a premises licence is not the holder of the licence, he may notify the relevant licensing authority under this subsection of any change in his name or address.

(5) Where the designated premises supervisor gives a notice under subsection (4), he must, as soon as is reasonably practicable, give the holder of the premises licence a copy of that notice.

(6) A person commits an offence if he fails, without reasonable excuse, to comply with this section.

(7) A person guilty of an offence under subsection (6) is liable on summary conviction to a fine not exceeding level 2 on the standard scale.

Variation of licences

34 Application to vary premises licence

(1) The holder of a premises licence may apply to the relevant licensing authority for variation of the licence.

(2) Subsection (1) is subject to regulations under—

(a) section 54 (form etc. of applications etc.);

(b) section 55 (fees to accompany applications etc.).

(3) An application under this section must also be accompanied by the premises licence (or the appropriate part of that licence) or, if that is not practicable, by a statement of the reasons for the failure to provide the licence (or part).

(4) This section does not apply to an application within section 37(1) (application to vary licence to specify individual as premises supervisor).

(5) The duty to make regulations imposed on the Secretary of State by subsection (5) of section 17 (advertisement etc. of application) applies in relation to applications under this section as it applies in relation to applications under that section.

35 Determination of application under section 34

(1) This section applies where the relevant licensing authority—

(a) receives an application, made in accordance with section 34, to vary a premises licence, and

(b) is satisfied that the applicant has complied with any requirement imposed on him by virtue of subsection (5) of that section.

(2) Subject to subsection (3) and section 36(6), the authority must grant the application.

(3) Where relevant representations are made, the authority must—

(a) hold a hearing to consider them, unless the authority, the applicant and each person who has made such representations agree that a hearing is unnecessary, and

(b) having regard to the representations, take such of the steps mentioned in subsection (4) (if any) as it considers necessary for the promotion of the licensing objectives.

(4) The steps are—

(a) to modify the conditions of the licence;

(b) to reject the whole or part of the application;

and for this purpose the conditions of the licence are modified if any of them is altered or omitted or any new condition is added.

(5) In this section "relevant representations" means representations which—

(a) are about the likely effect of the grant of the application on the promotion of the licensing objectives, and

(b) meet the requirements of subsection (6).

(6) The requirements are—

(a) that the representations are made by an interested party or responsible authority within the period prescribed under section 17(5)(c) by virtue of section 34(5),

(b) that they have not been withdrawn, and

(c) in the case of representations made by an interested party (who is not also a responsible authority), that they are not, in the opinion of the relevant licensing authority, frivolous or vexatious.

(7) Subsections (2) and (3) are subject to sections 19, 20 and 21 (which require certain conditions to be included in premises licences).

36 Supplementary provision about determinations under section 35

(1) Where an application (or any part of an application) is granted under section 35, the relevant licensing authority must forthwith give a notice to that effect to—

(a) the applicant,

(b) any person who made relevant representations in respect of the application, and

(c) the chief officer of police for the police area (or each police area) in which the premises are situated.

(2) Where relevant representations were made in respect of the application, the notice under subsection (1) must state the authority's reasons for its decision as to the steps (if any) to take under section 35(3)(b).

(3) The notice under subsection (1) must specify the time when the variation in question takes effect.

That time is the time specified in the application or, if that time is before the applicant is given that notice, such later time as the relevant licensing authority specifies in the notice.

(4) Where an application (or any part of an application) is rejected under section 35, the relevant licensing authority must forthwith give a notice to that effect stating its reasons for rejecting the application to—

(a) the applicant,

(b) any person who made relevant representations in respect of the application, and

(c) the chief officer of police for the police area (or each police area) in which the premises are situated.

(5) Where the relevant licensing authority determines for the purposes of section 35(6)(c) that any representations are frivolous or vexatious, it must notify the person who made them of the reasons for that determination.

(6) A licence may not be varied under section 35 so as—

(a) to extend the period for which the licence has effect, or

(b) to vary substantially the premises to which it relates.

(7) In discharging its duty under subsection (2) or (3)(b) of that section, a licensing authority may vary a premises licence so that it has effect subject to different conditions in respect of—

(a) different parts of the premises concerned;

(b) different licensable activities.

(8) In this section "relevant representations" has the meaning given in section 35(5).

37 Application to vary licence to specify individual as premises supervisor

(1) The holder of a premises licence may—

(a) if the licence authorises the supply of alcohol, or

(b) if he has applied under section 34 to vary the licence so that it authorises such supplies,

apply to vary the licence so as to specify the individual named in the application ("the proposed individual") as the premises supervisor.

(2) Subsection (1) is subject to regulations under—

(a) section 54 (form etc. of applications etc.);

(b) section 55 (fees to accompany applications etc.).

(3) An application under this section must also be accompanied by—

(a) a form of consent in the prescribed form given by the proposed individual, and

(b) the premises licence (or the appropriate part of that licence) or, if that is not practicable, a statement of the reasons for the failure to provide the licence (or part).

(4) The holder of the premises licence must give notice of his application—

(a) to the chief officer of police for the police area (or each police area) in which the premises are situated, and

(b) to the designated premises supervisor (if there is one),

and that notice must state whether the application is one to which section 38 applies.

(5) Where a chief officer of police notified under subsection (4) is satisfied that the exceptional circumstances of the case are such that granting the application would undermine the crime prevention objective, he must give the relevant licensing authority a notice stating the reasons why he is so satisfied.

(6) The chief officer of police must give that notice within the period of 14 days beginning with the day on which he is notified of the application under subsection (4).

38 Circumstances in which section 37 application given interim effect

(1) This section applies where an application made in accordance with section 37, in respect of a premises licence which authorises the supply of alcohol, includes a request that the variation applied for should have immediate effect.

(2) By virtue of this section, the premises licence has effect during the application period as if it were varied in the manner set out in the application.

(3) For this purpose "the application period" means the period which—

(a) begins when the application is received by the relevant licensing authority, and

(b) ends—

(i) if the application is granted, when the variation takes effect,

(ii) if the application is rejected, at the time the rejection is notified to the applicant, or

(iii) if the application is withdrawn before it is determined, at the time of the withdrawal.

39 Determination of section 37 application

(1) This section applies where an application is made, in accordance with section 37, to vary a premises licence so as to specify a new premises supervisor ("the proposed individual").

(2) Subject to subsection (3), the relevant licensing authority must grant the application.

(3) Where a notice is given under section 37(5) (and not withdrawn), the authority must—

(a) hold a hearing to consider it, unless the authority, the applicant and the chief officer of police who gave the notice agree that a hearing is unnecessary, and

(b) having regard to the notice, reject the application if it considers it necessary for the promotion of the crime prevention objective to do so.

(4) Where an application under section 37 is granted or rejected, the relevant licensing authority must give a notice to that effect to—

(a) the applicant,

(b) the proposed individual, and

(c) the chief officer of police for the police area (or each police area) in which the premises are situated.

(5) Where a chief officer of police gave a notice under subsection (5) of that section (and it was not withdrawn), the notice under subsection (4) of this section must state the authority's reasons for granting or rejecting the application.

(6) Where the application is granted, the notice under subsection (4) must specify the time when the variation takes effect.

That time is the time specified in the application or, if that time is before the applicant is given that notice, such later time as the relevant licensing authority specifies in the notice.

40 Duty of applicant following determination under section 39

(1) Where the holder of a premises licence is notified under section 39(4), he must forthwith—

(a) if his application has been granted, notify the person (if any) who has been replaced as the designated premises supervisor of the variation, and

(b) if his application has been rejected, give the designated premises supervisor (if any) notice to that effect.

(2) A person commits an offence if he fails, without reasonable excuse, to comply with subsection (1).

(3) A person guilty of an offence under subsection (2) is liable on summary conviction to a fine not exceeding level 3 on the standard scale.

41 Request to be removed as designated premises supervisor

(1) Where an individual wishes to cease being the designated premises supervisor in respect of a premises licence, he may give the relevant licensing authority a notice to that effect.

(2) Subsection (1) is subject to regulations under section 54 (form etc. of notices etc.).

(3) Where the individual is the holder of the premises licence, the notice under subsection (1) must also be accompanied by the premises licence (or the appropriate part of the licence) or, if that is not practicable, by a statement of the reasons for the failure to provide the licence (or part).

(4) In any other case, the individual must no later than 48 hours after giving the notice under subsection (1) give the holder of the premises licence—

(a) a copy of that notice, and

(b) a notice directing the holder to send to the relevant licensing authority within 14 days of receiving the notice—

(i) the premises licence (or the appropriate part of the licence), or

(ii) if that is not practicable, a statement of the reasons for the failure to provide the licence (or part).

(5) A person commits an offence if he fails, without reasonable excuse, to comply with a direction given to him under subsection (4)(b).

(6) A person guilty of an offence under subsection (5) is liable on summary conviction to a fine not exceeding level 3 on the standard scale.

(7) Where an individual—

(a) gives the relevant licensing authority a notice in accordance with this section, and

(b) satisfies the requirements of subsection (3) or (4),

he is to be treated for the purposes of this Act as if, from the relevant time, he were not the designated premises supervisor.

(8) For this purpose "the relevant time" means—

(a) the time the notice under subsection (1) is received by the relevant licensing authority, or

(b) if later, the time specified in the notice.

Transfer of premises licence

42 Application for transfer of premises licence

(1) Subject to this section, any person mentioned in section 16(1) (applicant for premises licence) may apply to the relevant licensing authority for the transfer of a premises licence to him.

(2) Where the applicant is an individual he must be aged 18 or over.

(3) Subsection (1) is subject to regulations under—

(a) section 54 (form etc. of applications etc.);

(b) section 55 (fees to accompany applications etc.).

(4) An application under this section must also be accompanied by the premises licence or, if that is not practicable, a statement of the reasons for the failure to provide the licence.

(5) The applicant must give notice of his application to the chief officer of police for the police area (or each police area) in which the premises are situated.

(6) Where a chief officer of police notified under subsection (5) is satisfied that the exceptional circumstances of the case are such that granting the application would undermine the crime prevention objective, he must give the relevant licensing authority a notice stating the reasons why he is so satisfied.

(7) The chief officer of police must give that notice within the period of 14 days beginning with the day on which he is notified of the application under subsection (5).

43 Circumstances in which transfer application given interim effect

(1) Where—

(a) an application made in accordance with section 42 includes a request that the transfer have immediate effect, and

(b) the requirements of this section are met,

then, by virtue of this section, the premises licence has effect during the application period as if the applicant were the holder of the licence.

(2) For this purpose "the application period" means the period which—

(a) begins when the application is received by the relevant licensing authority, and

(b) ends—

(i) when the licence is transferred following the grant of the application, or

(ii) if the application is rejected, when the applicant is notified of the rejection, or

(iii) when the application is withdrawn.

(3) Subject to subsections (4) and (5), an application within subsection (1)(a) may be made only with the consent of the holder of the premises licence.

(4) Where a person is the holder of the premises licence by virtue of an interim authority notice under section 47, such an application may also be made by that person.

(5) The relevant licensing authority must exempt the applicant from the requirement to obtain the holder's consent if the applicant shows to the authority's satisfaction—

(a) that he has taken all reasonable steps to obtain that consent, and

(b) that, if the application were one to which subsection (1) applied, he would be in a position to use the premises during the application period for the licensable activity or activities authorised by the premises licence.

(6) Where the relevant licensing authority refuses to exempt an applicant under subsection (5), it must notify the applicant of its reasons for that decision.

44 Determination of transfer application

(1) This section applies where an application for the transfer of a licence is made in accordance with section 42.

(2) Subject to subsections (3) and (5), the authority must transfer the licence in accordance with the application.

(3) The authority must reject the application if none of the conditions in subsection (4) applies.

(4) The conditions are—

(a) that section 43(1) (applications given interim effect) applies to the application,

(b) that the holder of the premises licence consents to the transfer,

(c) that the applicant is exempted under subsection (6) from the requirement to obtain the holder's consent to the transfer.

(5) Where a notice is given under section 42(6) (and not withdrawn), and subsection (3) above does not apply, the authority must—

(a) hold a hearing to consider it, unless the authority, the applicant and the chief officer of police who gave the notice agree that a hearing is unnecessary, and

(b) having regard to the notice, reject the application if it considers it necessary for the promotion of the crime prevention objective to do so.

(6) The relevant licensing authority must exempt the applicant from the requirement to obtain the holder's consent if the applicant shows to the authority's satisfaction—

(a) that he has taken all reasonable steps to obtain that consent, and

(b) that, if the application were granted, he would be in a position to use the premises for the licensable activity or activities authorised by the premises licence.

(7) Where the relevant licensing authority refuses to exempt an applicant under subsection (6), it must notify the applicant of its reasons for that decision.

45 Notification of determination under section 44

(1) Where an application under section 42 is granted or rejected, the relevant licensing authority must give a notice to that effect to—

(a) the applicant, and

(b) the chief officer of police for the police area (or each police area) in which the premises are situated.

(2) Where a chief officer of police gave a notice under subsection (6) of that section (and it was not withdrawn), the notice under subsection (1) of this section must state the licensing authority's reasons for granting or rejecting the application.

(3) Where the application is granted, the notice under subsection (1) must specify the time when the transfer takes effect.

That time is the time specified in the application or, if that time is before the applicant is given that notice, such later time as the relevant licensing authority specifies in the notice.

(4) The relevant licensing authority must also give a copy of the notice given under subsection (1)—

(a) where the application is granted—

(i) to the holder of the licence immediately before the application was granted, or

(ii) if the application was one to which section 43(1) applied, to the holder of the licence immediately before the application was made (if any),

(b) where the application is rejected, to the holder of the premises licence (if any).

46 Duty to notify designated premises supervisor of transfer

(1) This section applies where—

(a) an application is made in accordance with section 42 to transfer a premises licence in respect of which there is a designated premises supervisor, and

(b) the applicant and that supervisor are not the same person.

(2) Where section 43(1) applies in relation to the application, the applicant must forthwith notify the designated premises supervisor of the application.

(3) If the application is granted, the applicant must forthwith notify the designated premises supervisor of the transfer.

(4) A person commits an offence if he fails, without reasonable excuse, to comply with this section.

(5) A person guilty of an offence under subsection (4) is liable on summary conviction to a fine not exceeding level 3 on the standard scale.

Interim authority notices

47 Interim authority notice following death etc. of licence holder

(1) This section applies where—

(a) a premises licence lapses under section 27 in a case within subsection (1)(a), (b) or (c) of that section (death, incapacity or insolvency of the holder), but

(b) no application for transfer of the licence has been made by virtue of section 50 (reinstatement of licence on transfer following death etc.).

(2) A person who—

(a) has a prescribed interest in the premises concerned, or

(b) is connected to the person who held the premises licence immediately before it lapsed ("the former holder"),

may, during the initial seven day period, give to the relevant licensing authority a notice (an "interim authority notice") in respect of the licence.

(3) Subsection (2) is subject to regulations under—

(a) section 54 (form etc. of notices etc.);

(b) section 55 (fees to accompany applications etc.).

(4) Only one interim authority notice may be given under subsection (2).

(5) For the purposes of subsection (2) a person is connected to the former holder of the premises licence if, and only if—

(a) the former holder has died and that person is his personal representative,

(b) the former holder has become mentally incapable and that person acts for him under a power of attorney created by an instrument registered under section 6 of the Enduring Powers of Attorney Act 1985 (c. 29) , or

(c) the former holder has become insolvent and that person is his insolvency practitioner.

(6) Where an interim authority notice is given in accordance with this section—

(a) the premises licence is reinstated from the time the notice is received by the relevant licensing authority, and

(b) the person who gave the notice is from that time the holder of the licence.

(7) But the premises licence lapses again—

(a) at the end of the initial seven day period unless before that time the person who gave the interim authority notice has given a copy of the notice to the chief officer of police for the police area (or each police area) in which the premises are situated;

(b) at the end of the interim authority period, unless before that time a relevant transfer application is made to the relevant licensing authority.

(8) Nothing in this section prevents the person who gave the interim authority notice from making a relevant transfer application.

(9) If—

(a) a relevant transfer application is made during the interim authority period, and

(b) that application is rejected or withdrawn,

the licence lapses again at the time of the rejection or withdrawal.

(10) In this section—

"becomes insolvent" is to be construed in accordance with section 27;

"initial seven day period", in relation to a licence which lapses as mentioned in subsection (1), means the period of seven days beginning with the day after the day the licence lapses;

"insolvency practitioner", in relation to a person, means a person acting as an insolvency practitioner in relation to him (within the meaning of section 388 of the Insolvency Act 1986 (c. 45));

"interim authority period" means the period beginning with the day on which the interim authority notice is received by the relevant licensing authority and ending—

(a) two months after that day, or

(b) if earlier, when it is terminated by the person who gave the interim authority notice notifying the relevant licensing authority to that effect;

"mentally incapable" has the same meaning as in section 27(1)(b); and

"relevant transfer application" in relation to the premises licence, is an application under section 42 which is given interim effect by virtue of section 43.

48 Cancellation of interim authority notice following police objections

(1) This section applies where—

(a) an interim authority notice by a person ("the relevant person") is given in accordance with section 47,

(b) the chief officer of police for the police area (or each police area) in which the premises are situated is given a copy of the interim authority notice before the end of the initial seven day period (within the meaning of that section), and

(c) that chief officer (or any of those chief officers) is satisfied that the exceptional circumstances of the case are such that a failure to cancel the interim authority notice would undermine the crime prevention objective.

(2) The chief officer of police must no later than 48 hours after he receives the copy of the interim authority notice give the relevant licensing authority a notice stating why he is so satisfied.

(3) Where a notice is given by the chief officer of police (and not withdrawn), the authority must—

(a) hold a hearing to consider it, unless the authority, the relevant person and the chief officer of police agree that a hearing is unnecessary, and

(b) having regard to the notice given by the chief officer of police, cancel the interim authority notice if it considers it necessary for the promotion of the crime prevention objective to do so.

(4) An interim authority notice is cancelled under subsection (3)(b) by the licensing authority giving the relevant person a notice stating that it is cancelled and the authority's reasons for its decision.

(5) The licensing authority must give a copy of a notice under subsection (4) to the chief officer of police for the police area (or each police area) in which the premises are situated.

(6) The premises licence lapses if, and when, a notice is given under subsection (4).

This is subject to paragraph 7(5) of Schedule 5 (reinstatement of premises licence where appeal made against cancellation of interim authority notice).

(7) The relevant licensing authority must not cancel an interim authority notice after a relevant transfer application (within the meaning of section 47) is made in respect of the premises licence.

49 Supplementary provision about interim authority notices

(1) On receipt of an interim authority notice, the relevant licensing authority must issue to the person who gave the notice a copy of the licence and a copy of the summary (in each case certified by the authority to be a true copy).

(2) The copies issued under this section must be copies of the premises licence and summary in the form in which they existed immediately before the licence lapsed under section 27, except that they must specify the person who gave the interim authority notice as the person who is the holder.

(3) This Act applies in relation to a copy issued under this section as it applies in relation to an original licence or summary.

(4) Where a person becomes the holder of a premises licence by virtue of section 47, he must (unless he is the designated premises supervisor under the licence) forthwith notify the supervisor (if any) of the interim authority notice.

(5) A person commits an offence if he fails, without reasonable excuse, to comply with subsection (4).

(6) A person guilty of an offence under subsection (5) is liable on summary conviction to a fine not exceeding level 3 on the standard scale.

Transfer following death etc. of licence holder

50 Reinstatement of licence on transfer following death etc. of holder

(1) This section applies where—

(a) a premises licence lapses by virtue of section 27 (death, incapacity or insolvency etc. of the holder), but no interim authority notice has effect, or

(b) a premises licence lapses by virtue of section 28 (surrender).

(2) For the purposes of subsection (1)(a) an interim authority notice ceases to have effect when it is cancelled under section 48 or withdrawn.

(3) Notwithstanding the lapsing of the licence, a person mentioned in section 16(1) (who, in the case of an individual, is aged 18 or over) may apply under section 42 for the transfer of the licence to him provided that the application—

(a) is made no later than seven days after the day the licence lapsed, and

(b) is one to which section 43(1)(a) applies.

(4) Where an application is made in accordance with subsection (3), section 43(1)(b) must be disregarded.

(5) Where such an application is made, the premises licence is reinstated from the time the application is received by the relevant licensing authority.

(6) But the licence lapses again if, and when—

(a) the applicant is notified of the rejection of the application, or

(b) the application is withdrawn.

(7) Only one application for transfer of the premises licence may be made in reliance on this section.

Review of licences

51 Application for review of premises licence

(1) Where a premises licence has effect, an interested party or a responsible authority may apply to the relevant licensing authority for a review of the licence.

(2) Subsection (1) is subject to regulations under section 54 (form etc. of applications etc.).

(3) The Secretary of State must by regulations under this section—

(a) require the applicant to give a notice containing details of the application to the holder of the premises licence and each responsible authority within such period as may be prescribed;

(b) require the authority to advertise the application and invite representations about it to be made to the authority by interested parties and responsible authorities;

(c) prescribe the period during which representations may be made by the holder of the premises licence, any responsible authority or any interested party;

(d) require any notice under paragraph (a) or advertisement under paragraph (b) to specify that period.

(4) The relevant licensing authority may, at any time, reject any ground for review specified in an application under this section if it is satisfied—

(a) that the ground is not relevant to one or more of the licensing objectives, or

(b) in the case of an application made by a person other than a responsible authority, that—

(i) the ground is frivolous or vexatious, or

(ii) the ground is a repetition.

(5) For this purpose a ground for review is a repetition if—

(a) it is identical or substantially similar to—

(i) a ground for review specified in an earlier application for review made in respect of the same premises licence and determined under section 52, or

(ii) representations considered by the relevant licensing authority in accordance with section 18, before it determined the application for the premises licence under that section, or

(iii) representations which would have been so considered but for the fact that they were excluded representations by virtue of section 32, and

(b) a reasonable interval has not elapsed since that earlier application for review or the grant of the licence (as the case may be).

(6) Where the authority rejects a ground for review under subsection (4)(b), it must notify the applicant of its decision and, if the ground was rejected because it was frivolous or vexatious, the authority must notify him of its reasons for making that decision.

(7) The application is to be treated as rejected to the extent that any of the grounds for review are rejected under subsection (4).

Accordingly the requirements imposed under subsection (3)(a) and (b) and by section 52 (so far as not already met) apply only to so much (if any) of the application as has not been rejected.

52 Determination of application for review

(1) This section applies where—

(a) the relevant licensing authority receives an application made in accordance with section 51,

(b) the applicant has complied with any requirement imposed on him under subsection (3)(a) or (d) of that section, and

(c) the authority has complied with any requirement imposed on it under subsection (3)(b) or (d) of that section.

(2) Before determining the application, the authority must hold a hearing to consider it and any relevant representations.

(3) The authority must, having regard to the application and any relevant representations, take such of the steps mentioned in subsection (4) (if any) as it considers necessary for the promotion of the licensing objectives.

(4) The steps are—

(a) to modify the conditions of the licence;

(b) to exclude a licensable activity from the scope of the licence;

(c) to remove the designated premises supervisor;

(d) to suspend the licence for a period not exceeding three months;

(e) to revoke the licence;

and for this purpose the conditions of the licence are modified if any of them is altered or omitted or any new condition is added.

(5) Subsection (3) is subject to sections 19, 20 and 21 (requirement to include certain conditions in premises licences).

(6) Where the authority takes a step mentioned in subsection (4)(a) or (b), it may provide that the modification or exclusion is to have effect for only such period (not exceeding three months) as it may specify.

(7) In this section "relevant representations" means representations which—
- (a) are relevant to one or more of the licensing objectives, and
- (b) meet the requirements of subsection (8).

(8) The requirements are—
- (a) that the representations are made—
  - (i) by the holder of the premises licence, a responsible authority or an interested party, and
  - (ii) within the period prescribed under section 51(3)(c),
- (b) that they have not been withdrawn, and
- (c) if they are made by an interested party (who is not also a responsible authority), that they are not, in the opinion of the relevant licensing authority, frivolous or vexatious.

(9) Where the relevant licensing authority determines that any representations are frivolous or vexatious, it must notify the person who made them of the reasons for that determination.

(10) Where a licensing authority determines an application for review under this section it must notify the determination and its reasons for making it to—
- (a) the holder of the licence,
- (b) the applicant,
- (c) any person who made relevant representations, and
- (d) the chief officer of police for the police area (or each police area) in which the premises are situated.

(11) A determination under this section does not have effect—
- (a) until the end of the period given for appealing against the decision, or
- (b) if the decision is appealed against, until the appeal is disposed of.

53 Supplementary provision about review

(1) This section applies where a local authority is both—
- (a) the relevant licensing authority, and
- (b) a responsible authority,

in respect of any premises.

(2) The authority may, in its capacity as a responsible authority, apply under section 51 for a review of any premises licence in respect of the premises.

(3) The authority may, in its capacity as licensing authority, determine that application.

General provision

54 Form etc. of applications and notices under Part 3

In relation to any application or notice under this Part, regulations may prescribe—

(a) its form;
(b) the manner in which it is to be made or given;
(c) information and documents that must accompany it.

55 Fees

(1) Regulations may—
(a) require applications under any provision of this Part (other than section 51) or notices under section 47 to be accompanied by a fee, and
(b) prescribe the amount of the fee.

(2) Regulations may also require the holder of a premises licence to pay the relevant licensing authority an annual fee.

(3) Regulations under subsection (2) may include provision prescribing—
(a) the amount of the fee, and
(b) the time at which any such fee is due.

(4) Any fee which is owed to a licensing authority under subsection (2) may be recovered as a debt due to the authority.

Production of licence, rights of entry, etc.

56 Licensing authority's duty to update licence document

(1) Where—
(a) the relevant licensing authority, in relation to a premises licence, makes a determination or receives a notice under this Part,
(b) a premises licence lapses under this Part, or
(c) an appeal against a decision under this Part is disposed of,

the relevant licensing authority must make the appropriate amendments (if any) to the licence and, if necessary, issue a new summary of the licence.

(2) Where a licensing authority is not in possession of the licence (or the appropriate part of the licence) it may, for the purposes of discharging its obligations under subsection (1), require the holder of a premises licence to produce the licence (or the appropriate part) to the authority within 14 days from the date on which he is notified of the requirement.

(3) A person commits an offence if he fails, without reasonable excuse, to comply with a requirement under subsection (2).

(4) A person guilty of an offence under subsection (3) is liable on summary conviction to a fine not exceeding level 2 on the standard scale.

57 Duty to keep and produce licence

(1) This section applies whenever premises in respect of which a premises licence has effect are being used for one or more licensable activities authorised by the licence.

(2) The holder of the premises licence must secure that the licence or a certified copy of it is kept at the premises in the custody or under the control of—

(a) the holder of the licence, or

(b) a person who works at the premises and whom the holder of the licence has nominated in writing for the purposes of this subsection.

(3) The holder of the premises licence must secure that—

(a) the summary of the licence or a certified copy of that summary, and

(b) a notice specifying the position held at the premises by any person nominated for the purposes of subsection (2),

are prominently displayed at the premises.

(4) The holder of a premises licence commits an offence if he fails, without reasonable excuse, to comply with subsection (2) or (3).

(5) A constable or an authorised person may require the person who, by virtue of arrangements made for the purposes of subsection (2), is required to have the premises licence (or a certified copy of it) in his custody or under his control to produce the licence (or such a copy) for examination.

(6) An authorised person exercising the power conferred by subsection (5) must, if so requested, produce evidence of his authority to exercise the power.

(7) A person commits an offence if he fails, without reasonable excuse, to produce a premises licence or certified copy of a premises licence in accordance with a requirement under subsection (5).

(8) A person guilty of an offence under this section is liable on summary conviction to a fine not exceeding level 2 on the standard scale.

(9) In subsection (3) the reference to the summary of the licence is a reference to the summary issued under section 23 or, where one or more summaries have subsequently been issued under section 56, the most recent summary to have been so issued.

(10) Section 58 makes provision about certified copies of documents for the purposes of this section.

58 Provision supplementary to section 57

(1) Any reference in section 57 to a certified copy of any document is a reference to a copy of that document which is certified to be a true copy by—

(a) the relevant licensing authority,

(b) a solicitor or notary, or

(c) a person of a prescribed description.

(2) Any certified copy produced in accordance with a requirement under section 57(5) must be a copy of the document in the form in which it exists at the time.

(3) A document which purports to be a certified copy of a document is to be taken to be such a copy, and to comply with the requirements of subsection (2), unless the contrary is shown.

59 Inspection of premises before grant of licence etc.

(1) In this section "relevant application" means an application under—

(a) section 17 (grant of licence),

(b) section 29 (provisional statement),
(c) section 34 (variation of licence), or
(d) section 51 (review of licence).

(2) A constable or an authorised person may, at any reasonable time before the determination of a relevant application, enter the premises to which the application relates to assess—
(a) in a case within subsection (1)(a), (b) or (c), the likely effect of the grant of the application on the promotion of the licensing objectives, and
(b) in a case within subsection (1)(d), the effect of the activities authorised by the premises licence on the promotion of those objectives.

(3) An authorised person exercising the power conferred by this section must, if so requested, produce evidence of his authority to exercise the power.

(4) A constable or an authorised person exercising the power conferred by this section in relation to an application within subsection (1)(d) may, if necessary, use reasonable force.

(5) A person commits an offence if he intentionally obstructs an authorised person exercising a power conferred by this section.

(6) A person guilty of an offence under this section is liable on summary conviction to a fine not exceeding level 2 on the standard scale.

PART 4

CLUBS

Introductory

60 Club premises certificate

(1) In this Act "club premises certificate" means a certificate granted under this Part—
(a) in respect of premises occupied by, and habitually used for the purposes of, a club,
(b) by the relevant licensing authority, and
(c) certifying the matters specified in subsection (2).

(2) Those matters are—
(a) that the premises may be used by the club for one or more qualifying club activities specified in the certificate, and
(b) that the club is a qualifying club in relation to each of those activities (see section 61).

Qualifying clubs

61 Qualifying clubs

(1) This section applies for determining for the purposes of this Part whether a club is a qualifying club in relation to a qualifying club activity.

(2) A club is a qualifying club in relation to the supply of alcohol to members or guests if it satisfies both—

(a) the general conditions in section 62, and

(b) the additional conditions in section 64.

(3) A club is a qualifying club in relation to the provision of regulated entertainment if it satisfies the general conditions in section 62.

62 The general conditions

(1) The general conditions which a club must satisfy if it is to be a qualifying club in relation to a qualifying club activity are the following.

(2) Condition 1 is that under the rules of the club persons may not—

(a) be admitted to membership, or

(b) be admitted, as candidates for membership, to any of the privileges of membership,

without an interval of at least two days between their nomination or application for membership and their admission.

(3) Condition 2 is that under the rules of the club persons becoming members without prior nomination or application may not be admitted to the privileges of membership without an interval of at least two days between their becoming members and their admission.

(4) Condition 3 is that the club is established and conducted in good faith as a club (see section 63).

(5) Condition 4 is that the club has at least 25 members.

(6) Condition 5 is that alcohol is not supplied, or intended to be supplied, to members on the premises otherwise than by or on behalf of the club.

63 Determining whether a club is established and conducted in good faith

(1) In determining for the purposes of condition 3 in subsection (4) of section 62 whether a club is established and conducted in good faith as a club, the matters to be taken into account are those specified in subsection (2).

(2) Those matters are—

(a) any arrangements restricting the club's freedom of purchase of alcohol;

(b) any provision in the rules, or arrangements, under which—

(i) money or property of the club, or

(ii) any gain arising from the carrying on of the club,

is or may be applied otherwise than for the benefit of the club as a whole or for charitable, benevolent or political purposes;

(c) the arrangements for giving members information about the finances of the club;

(d) the books of account and other records kept to ensure the accuracy of that information;

(e) the nature of the premises occupied by the club.

(3) If a licensing authority decides for any purpose of this Act that a club does not satisfy condition 3 in subsection (4) of section 62, the authority must give the club notice of the decision and of the reasons for it.

64 The additional conditions for the supply of alcohol

(1) The additional conditions which a club must satisfy if it is to be a qualifying club in relation to the supply of alcohol to members or guests are the following.

(2) Additional condition 1 is that (so far as not managed by the club in general meeting or otherwise by the general body of members) the purchase of alcohol for the club, and the supply of alcohol by the club, are managed by a committee whose members—

- (a) are members of the club;
- (b) have attained the age of 18 years; and
- (c) are elected by the members of the club.

This subsection is subject to section 65 (which makes special provision for industrial and provident societies, friendly societies etc.).

(3) Additional condition 2 is that no arrangements are, or are intended to be, made for any person to receive at the expense of the club any commission, percentage or similar payment on, or with reference to, purchases of alcohol by the club.

(4) Additional condition 3 is that no arrangements are, or are intended to be, made for any person directly or indirectly to derive any pecuniary benefit from the supply of alcohol by or on behalf of the club to members or guests, apart from—

- (a) any benefit accruing to the club as a whole, or
- (b) any benefit which a person derives indirectly by reason of the supply giving rise or contributing to a general gain from the carrying on of the club.

65 Industrial and provident societies, friendly societies etc.

(1) Subsection (2) applies in relation to any club which is—

- (a) a registered society, within the meaning of the Industrial and Provident Societies Act 1965 (c. 12)(see section 74(1) of that Act),
- (b) a registered society, within the meaning of the Friendly Societies Act 1974 (c. 46) (see section 111(1) of that Act), or
- (c) a registered friendly society, within the meaning of the Friendly Societies Act 1992 (c. 40) (see section 116 of that Act).

(2) Any such club is to be taken for the purposes of this Act to satisfy additional condition 1 in subsection (2) of section 64 if and to the extent that—

- (a) the purchase of alcohol for the club, and
- (b) the supply of alcohol by the club,

are under the control of the members or of a committee appointed by the members.

(3) References in this Act, other than this section, to—

- (a) subsection (2) of section 64, or
- (b) additional condition 1 in that subsection,

are references to it as read with subsection (1) of this section.

(4) Subject to subsection (5), this Act applies in relation to an incorporated friendly society as it applies in relation to a club, and accordingly—

(a) the premises of the society are to be treated as the premises of a club,

(b) the members of the society are to be treated as the members of the club, and

(c) anything done by or on behalf of the society is to be treated as done by or on behalf of the club.

(5) In determining for the purposes of section 61 whether an incorporated friendly society is a qualifying club in relation to a qualifying club activity, the society is to be taken to satisfy the following conditions—

(a) condition 3 in subsection (4) of section 62,

(b) condition 5 in subsection (6) of that section,

(c) the additional conditions in section 64.

(6) In this section "incorporated friendly society" has the same meaning as in the Friendly Societies Act 1992 (see section 116 of that Act).

66 Miners' welfare institutes

(1) Subject to subsection (2), this Act applies to a relevant miners' welfare institute as it applies to a club, and accordingly—

(a) the premises of the institute are to be treated as the premises of a club,

(b) the persons enrolled as members of the institute are to be treated as the members of the club, and

(c) anything done by or on behalf of the trustees or managers in carrying on the institute is to be treated as done by or on behalf of the club.

(2) In determining for the purposes of section 61 whether a relevant miners' welfare institute is a qualifying club in relation to a qualifying club activity, the institute is to be taken to satisfy the following conditions—

(a) condition 3 in subsection (4) of section 62,

(b) condition 4 in subsection (5) of that section,

(c) condition 5 in subsection (6) of that section,

(d) the additional conditions in section 64.

(3) For the purposes of this section—

(a) "miners' welfare institute" means an association organised for the social well-being and recreation of persons employed in or about coal mines (or of such persons in particular), and

(b) a miners' welfare institute is "relevant" if it satisfies one of the following conditions.

(4) The first condition is that—

(a) the institute is managed by a committee or board, and

(b) at least two thirds of the committee or board consists—

(i) partly of persons appointed or nominated, or appointed or elected from among persons nominated, by one or more licensed operators within the meaning of the Coal Industry Act 1994 (c. 21), and

(ii) partly of persons appointed or nominated, or appointed or elected from among persons nominated, by one or more organisations representing persons employed in or about coal mines.

(5) The second condition is that—

(a) the institute is managed by a committee or board, but

(b) the making of—

(i) an appointment or nomination falling within subsection (4)(b)(i), or

(ii) an appointment or nomination falling within subsection (4)(b)(ii),

is not practicable or would not be appropriate, and

(c) at least two thirds of the committee or board consists—

(i) partly of persons employed, or formerly employed, in or about coal mines, and

(ii) partly of persons appointed by the Coal Industry Social Welfare Organisation or a body or person to which the functions of that Organisation have been transferred under section 12(3) of the Miners' Welfare Act 1952 (c. 23).

(6) The third condition is that the premises of the institute are held on trusts to which section 2 of the Recreational Charities Act 1958 (c. 17) applies.

Interpretation

67 Associate members and their guests

(1) Any reference in this Act (other than this section) to a guest of a member of a club includes a reference to—

(a) an associate member of the club, and

(b) a guest of an associate member of the club.

(2) For the purposes of this Act a person is an "associate member" of a club if—

(a) in accordance with the rules of the club, he is admitted to its premises as being a member of another club, and

(b) that other club is a recognised club (see section 193).

68 The relevant licensing authority

(1) For the purposes of this Part the "relevant licensing authority" in relation to any premises is determined in accordance with this section.

(2) Subject to subsection (3), the relevant licensing authority is the authority in whose area the premises are situated.

(3) Where the premises are situated in the areas of two or more licensing authorities, the relevant licensing authority is—

(a) the licensing authority in whose area the greater or greatest part of the premises is situated, or

(b) if there is no authority to which paragraph (a) applies, such one of those authorities as is nominated in accordance with subsection (4).

(4) In a case within subsection (3)(b), an applicant for a club premises certificate must nominate one of the licensing authorities as the relevant licensing authority in relation to the application and any certificate granted as a result of it.

69 Authorised persons, interested parties and responsible authorities

(1) In this Part in relation to any premises each of the following expressions has the meaning given to it by this section—

"authorised person",

"interested party",

"responsible authority".

(2) "Authorised person" means any of the following—

(a) an officer of a licensing authority in whose area the premises are situated who is authorised by that authority for the purposes of this Act,

(b) an inspector appointed under section 18 of the Fire Precautions Act 1971 (c. 40),

(c) an inspector appointed under section 19 of the Health and Safety at Work etc. Act 1974 (c. 37),

(d) an officer of a local authority, in whose area the premises are situated, who is authorised by that authority for the purposes of exercising one or more of its statutory functions in relation to minimising or preventing the risk of pollution of the environment or of harm to human health,

(e) in relation to a vessel, an inspector, or a surveyor of ships, appointed under section 256 of the Merchant Shipping Act 1995 (c. 21),

(f) a person prescribed for the purposes of this subsection.

(3) "Interested party" means any of the following—

(a) a person living in the vicinity of the premises,

(b) a body representing persons who live in that vicinity,

(c) a person involved in a business in that vicinity,

(d) a body representing persons involved in such businesses.

(4) "Responsible authority" means any of the following—

(a) the chief officer of police for any police area in which the premises are situated,

(b) the fire authority for any area in which the premises are situated,

(c) the enforcing authority within the meaning given by section 18 of the Health and Safety at Work etc. Act 1974 (c. 37) for any area in which the premises are situated,

(d) the local planning authority within the meaning given by the Town and Country Planning Act 1990 (c. 8) for any area in which the premises are situated,

(e) the local authority by which statutory functions are exercisable in any area in which the premises are situated in relation to minimising or preventing the risk of pollution of the environment or of harm to human health,

(f) a body which—

(i) represents those who, in relation to any such area, are responsible for, or interested in, matters relating to the protection of children from harm, and

(ii) is recognised by the licensing authority for that area for the purposes of this section as being competent to advise it on such matters,

(g) any licensing authority (other than the relevant licensing authority) in whose area part of the premises is situated,

(h) in relation to a vessel—

(i) a navigation authority (within the meaning of section 221(1) of the Water Resources Act 1991 (c. 57)) having functions in relation to the waters where the vessel is usually moored or berthed or any waters where it is, or is proposed to be, navigated at a time when it is used for qualifying club activities,

(ii) the Environment Agency,

(iii) the British Waterways Board, or

(iv) the Secretary of State,

(i) a person prescribed for the purposes of this subsection.

(5) For the purposes of this section, "statutory function" means a function conferred by or under any enactment.

70 Other definitions relating to clubs

In this Part—

"secretary", in relation to a club, includes any person (whether or not an officer of the club) performing the duties of a secretary;

"supply of alcohol to members or guests" means, in the case of any club,—

(a) the supply of alcohol by or on behalf of the club to, or to the order of, a member of the club, or

(b) the sale by retail of alcohol by or on behalf of the club to a guest of a member of the club for consumption on the premises where the sale takes place,

and related expressions are to be construed accordingly.

Grant of club premises certificate

71 Application for club premises certificate

(1) A club may apply for a club premises certificate in respect of any premises which are occupied by, and habitually used for the purposes of, the club.

(2) Any application for a club premises certificate must be made to the relevant licensing authority.

(3) Subsection (2) is subject to regulations under—

(a) section 91 (form etc. of applications and notices under this Part);

(b) section 92 (fees to accompany applications and notices).

(4) An application under this section must also be accompanied by—

(a) a club operating schedule,

(b) a plan of the premises to which the application relates, in the prescribed form, and

(c) a copy of the rules of the club.

(5) A "club operating schedule" is a document which is in the prescribed form, and includes a statement of the following matters—

(a) the qualifying club activities to which the application relates ("the relevant qualifying club activities"),

(b) the times during which it is proposed that the relevant qualifying club activities are to take place,

(c) any other times during which it is proposed that the premises are to be open to members and their guests,

(d) where the relevant qualifying club activities include the supply of alcohol, whether the supplies are proposed to be for consumption on the premises or both on and off the premises,

(e) the steps which it is proposed to take to promote the licensing objectives, and

(f) such other matters as may be prescribed.

(6) The Secretary of State must by regulations—

(a) require an applicant to advertise the application within the prescribed period—

(i) in the prescribed form, and

(ii) in a manner which is prescribed and is likely to bring the application to the attention of the interested parties likely to be affected by it;

(b) require an applicant to give notice of the application to each responsible authority, and such other persons as may be prescribed within the prescribed period;

(c) prescribe the period during which interested parties and responsible authorities may make representations to the relevant licensing authority about the application.

72 Determination of application for club premises certificate

(1) This section applies where the relevant licensing authority—

(a) receives an application for a club premises certificate made in accordance with section 71, and

(b) is satisfied that the applicant has complied with any requirement imposed on the applicant under subsection (6) of that section.

(2) Subject to subsection (3), the authority must grant the certificate in accordance with the application subject only to—

(a) such conditions as are consistent with the club operating schedule accompanying the application, and

(b) any conditions which must under section 73(2) to (5) or 74 be included in the certificate.

(3) Where relevant representations are made, the authority must—

(a) hold a hearing to consider them, unless the authority, the applicant and each person who has made such representations agree that a hearing is unnecessary, and

(b) having regard to the representations, take such of the steps mentioned in subsection (4) (if any) as it considers necessary for the promotion of the licensing objectives.

(4) The steps are—

(a) to grant the certificate subject to—

(i) the conditions mentioned in subsection (2)(a) modified to such extent as the authority considers necessary for the promotion of the licensing objectives, and

(ii) any conditions which must under section 73(2) to (5) or 74 be included in the certificate;

(b) to exclude from the scope of the certificate any of the qualifying club activities to which the application relates;

(c) to reject the application.

(5) Subsections (2) and (3)(b) are subject to section 73(1) (certificate may authorise off-supplies only if it authorises on-supplies).

(6) For the purposes of subsection (4)(a)(4)(a) the conditions mentioned in subsection (2)(a) are modified if any of them is altered or omitted or any new condition is added.

(7) For the purposes of this section, "relevant representations" means representations which—

(a) are about the likely effect of the grant of the certificate on the promotion of the licensing objectives, and

(b) meet the requirements of subsection (8).

(8) The requirements are—

(a) that the representations were made by an interested party or responsible authority within the period prescribed under section 71(6)(c),

(b) that they have not been withdrawn, and

(c) in the case of representations made by an interested party (who is not also a responsible authority), that they are not, in the opinion of the relevant licensing authority, frivolous or vexatious.

(9) Where the authority determines for the purposes of subsection (8)(c) that any representations are frivolous or vexatious, it must notify the person who made them of the reasons for its determination.

(10) In discharging its duty under subsection (2) or (3)(b) a licensing authority may grant a club premises certificate subject to different conditions in respect of—

(a) different parts of the premises concerned;

(b) different qualifying club activities.

73 Certificate authorising supply of alcohol for consumption off the premises

(1) A club premises certificate may not authorise the supply of alcohol for consumption off the premises unless it also authorises the supply of alcohol to a member of the club for consumption on those premises.

(2) A club premises certificate which authorises the supply of alcohol for consumption off the premises must include the following conditions.

(3) The first condition is that the supply must be made at a time when the premises are open for the purposes of supplying alcohol, in accordance with the club premises certificate, to members of the club for consumption on the premises.

(4) The second condition is that any alcohol supplied for consumption off the premises must be in a sealed container.

(5) The third condition is that any supply of alcohol for consumption off the premises must be made to a member of the club in person.

74 Mandatory condition: exhibition of films

(1) Where a club premises certificate authorises the exhibition of films, the certificate must include a condition requiring the admission of children to the exhibition of any film to be restricted in accordance with this section.

(2) Where the film classification body is specified in the certificate, unless subsection (3)(b) applies, admission of children must be restricted in accordance with any recommendation made by that body.

(3) Where—

(a) the film classification body is not specified in the certificate, or

(b) the relevant licensing authority has notified the club which holds the certificate that this subsection applies to the film in question,

admission of children must be restricted in accordance with any recommendation made by that licensing authority.

(4) In this section—

"children" means persons aged under 18; and

"film classification body" means the person or persons designated as the authority under section 4 of the Video Recordings Act 1984 (c. 39) (authority to determine suitability of video works for classification).

75 Prohibited conditions: associate members and their guests

(1) Where the rules of a club provide for the sale by retail of alcohol on any premises by or on behalf of the club to, or to a guest of, an associate member of the club, no condition may be attached to a club premises certificate in respect of the sale by retail of alcohol on those premises by or on behalf of the club so as to prevent the sale by retail of alcohol to any such associate member or guest.

(2) Where the rules of a club provide for the provision of any regulated entertainment on any premises by or on behalf of the club to, or to a guest of, an associate member of the club, no condition may be attached to a club premises certificate in respect of the provision of any such regulated entertainment on those premises by or on behalf of the club so as to prevent its provision to any such associate member or guest.

76 Prohibited conditions: plays

(1) In relation to a club premises certificate which authorises the performance of plays, no condition may be attached to the certificate as to the nature of the plays which may be performed, or the manner of performing plays, under the certificate.

(2) But subsection (1) does not prevent a licensing authority imposing, in accordance with section 72(2) or (3)(b), 85(3)(b) or 88(3), any condition which it considers necessary on the grounds of public safety.

77 Grant or rejection of application for club premises certificate

(1) Where an application is granted under section 72, the relevant licensing authority must forthwith—

(a) give a notice to that effect to—

(i) the applicant,

(ii) any person who made relevant representations in respect of the application, and

(iii) the chief officer of police for the police area (or each police area) in which the premises are situated, and

(b) issue the club with the club premises certificate and a summary of it.

(2) Where relevant representations were made in respect of the application, the notice under subsection (1)(a) must specify the authority's reasons for its decision as to the steps (if any) to take under section 72(3)(b).

(3) Where an application is rejected under section 72, the relevant licensing authority must forthwith give a notice to that effect, stating its reasons for that decision, to—

(a) the applicant,

(b) any person who made relevant representations in respect of the application, and

(c) the chief officer of police for the police area (or each police area) in which the premises are situated.

(4) In this section "relevant representations" has the meaning given in section 72(6).

78 Form of certificate and summary

(1) A club premises certificate and the summary of such a certificate must be in the prescribed form.

(2) Regulations under subsection (1) must, in particular, provide for the certificate to—

(a) specify the name of the club and the address which is to be its relevant registered address, as defined in section 184(7);

(b) specify the address of the premises to which the certificate relates;

(c) include a plan of those premises;

(d) specify the qualifying club activities for which the premises may be used;

(e) specify the conditions subject to which the certificate has effect.

79 Theft, loss, etc. of certificate or summary

(1) Where a club premises certificate or summary is lost, stolen, damaged or destroyed, the club may apply to the relevant licensing authority for a copy of the certificate or summary.

(2) Subsection (1) is subject to regulations under section 92(1) (power to prescribe fee to accompany application).

(3) Where an application is made in accordance with this section, the relevant licensing authority must issue the club with a copy of the certificate or summary (certified by the authority to be a true copy) if it is satisfied that—

(a) the certificate or summary has been lost, stolen, damaged or destroyed, and

(b) where it has been lost or stolen, the club has reported the loss or theft to the police.

(4) The copy issued under this section must be a copy of the club premises certificate or summary in the form in which it existed immediately before it was lost, stolen, damaged or destroyed.

(5) This Act applies in relation to a copy issued under this section as it applies in relation to an original club premises certificate or summary.

Duration of certificate

80 Period of validity of club premises certificate

(1) A club premises certificate has effect until such time as—

(a) it is withdrawn under section 88 or 90, or

(b) it lapses by virtue of section 81(3) (surrender).

(2) But a club premises certificate does not have effect during any period when it is suspended under section 88.

81 Surrender of club premises certificate

(1) Where a club which holds a club premises certificate decides to surrender it, the club may give the relevant licensing authority a notice to that effect.

(2) The notice must be accompanied by the club premises certificate or, if that is not practicable, by a statement of the reasons for the failure to produce the certificate.

(3) Where a notice is given in accordance with this section, the certificate lapses on receipt of the notice by the authority.

Duty to notify certain changes

82 Notification of change of name or alteration of rules of club

(1) Where a club—

(a) holds a club premises certificate, or

(b) has made an application for a club premises certificate which has not been determined by the relevant licensing authority,

the secretary of the club must give the relevant licensing authority notice of any change in the name, or alteration made to the rules, of the club.

(2) Subsection (1) is subject to regulations under section 92(1) (power to prescribe fee to accompany application).

(3) A notice under subsection (1) by a club which holds a club premises certificate must be accompanied by the certificate or, if that is not practicable, by a statement of the reasons for the failure to produce the certificate.

(4) An authority notified under this section of a change in the name, or alteration to the rules, of a club must amend the club premises certificate accordingly.

(5) But nothing in subsection (4) requires or authorises the making of any amendment to a club premises certificate so as to change the premises to which the certificate relates (and no amendment made under that subsection to a club premises certificate has effect so as to change those premises).

(6) If a notice required by this section is not given within the 28 days following the day on which the change of name or alteration to the rules is made, the secretary of the club commits an offence.

(7) A person guilty of an offence under subsection (6) is liable on summary conviction to a fine not exceeding level 2 on the standard scale.

83 Change of relevant registered address of club

(1) A club which holds a club premises certificate may give the relevant licensing authority notice of any change desired to be made in the address which is to be the club's relevant registered address.

(2) If a club which holds a club premises certificate ceases to have any authority to make use of the address which is its relevant registered address, it must as soon as reasonably practicable give to the relevant licensing authority notice of the change to be made in the address which is to be the club's relevant registered address.

(3) Subsections (1) and (2) are subject to regulations under section 92(1) (power to prescribe fee to accompany application).

(4) A notice under subsection (1) or (2) must also be accompanied by the club premises certificate or, if that is not practicable, by a statement of the reasons for the failure to produce the certificate.

(5) An authority notified under subsection (1) or (2) of a change to be made in the relevant registered address of a club must amend the club premises certificate accordingly.

(6) If a club fails, without reasonable excuse, to comply with subsection (2) the secretary commits an offence.

(7) A person guilty of an offence under subsection (6) is liable on summary conviction to a fine not exceeding level 2 on the standard scale.

(8) In this section "relevant registered address" has the meaning given in section 184(7).

Variation of certificates

84 Application to vary club premises certificate

(1) A club which holds a club premises certificate may apply to the relevant licensing authority for variation of the certificate.

(2) Subsection (1) is subject to regulations under—
   (a) section 91 (form etc. of applications);
   (b) section 92 (fees to accompany applications).

(3) An application under this section must also be accompanied by the club premises certificate or, if that is not practicable, by a statement of the reasons for the failure to provide the certificate.

(4) The duty to make regulations imposed on the Secretary of State by subsection (6) of section 71 (advertisement etc. of application) applies in relation to applications under this section as it applies in relation to applications under that section.

85 Determination of application under section 84

(1) This section applies where the relevant licensing authority—

(a) receives an application, made in accordance with section 84, to vary a club premises certificate, and

(b) is satisfied that the applicant has complied with any requirement imposed by virtue of subsection (4) of that section.

(2) Subject to subsection (3) and section 86(6), the authority must grant the application.

(3) Where relevant representations are made, the authority must—

(a) hold a hearing to consider them, unless the authority, the applicant and each person who has made such representations agree that a hearing is unnecessary, and

(b) having regard to the representations, take such of the steps mentioned in subsection (4) (if any) as it considers necessary for the promotion of the licensing objectives.

(4) The steps are—

(a) to modify the conditions of the certificate;

(b) to reject the whole or part of the application;

and for this purpose the conditions of the certificate are modified if any of them is altered or omitted or any new condition is added.

(5) In this section "relevant representations" means representations which—

(a) are about the likely effect of the grant of the application on the promotion of the licensing objectives, and

(b) meet the requirements of subsection (6).

(6) The requirements are—

(a) that the representations are made by an interested party or responsible authority within the period prescribed under section 71(6)(c) by virtue of section 84(4),

(b) that they have not been withdrawn, and

(c) in the case of representations made by an interested party (who is not also a responsible authority), that they are not, in the opinion of the relevant licensing authority, frivolous or vexatious.

(7) Subsections (2) and (3) are subject to sections 73 and 74 (mandatory conditions relating to supply of alcohol for consumption off the premises and to exhibition of films).

86 Supplementary provision about applications under section 84

(1) Where an application (or any part of an application) is granted under section 85, the relevant licensing authority must forthwith give a notice to that effect to—

(a) the applicant,

(b) any person who made relevant representations in respect of the application, and

(c) the chief officer of police for the police area (or each police area) in which the premises are situated.

(2) Where relevant representations were made in respect of the application, the notice under subsection (1) must specify the authority's reasons for its decision as to the steps (if any) to take under section 85(3)(b).

(3) The notice under subsection (1) must specify the time when the variation in question takes effect.

That time is the time specified in the application or, if that time is before the applicant is given the notice, such later time as the relevant licensing authority specifies in the notice.

(4) Where an application (or any part of an application) is rejected under section 85, the relevant licensing authority must forthwith give a notice to that effect stating its reasons for rejecting the application to—

(a) the applicant,

(b) any person who made relevant representations, and

(c) the chief officer of police for the police area (or each police area) in which the premises are situated.

(5) Where the relevant licensing authority determines for the purposes of section 85(6)(c) that any representations are frivolous or vexatious, it must give the person who made them its reasons for that determination.

(6) A club premises certificate may not be varied under section 85 so as to vary substantially the premises to which it relates.

(7) In discharging its duty under subsection (2) or (3)(b) of that section, a licensing authority may vary a club premises certificate so that it has effect subject to different conditions in respect of—

(a) different parts of the premises concerned;

(b) different qualifying club activities.

(8) In this section "relevant representations" has the meaning given in section 85(5).

Review of certificates

87 Application for review of club premises certificate

(1) Where a club holds a club premises certificate—

(a) an interested party,

(b) a responsible authority, or

(c) a member of the club,

may apply to the relevant licensing authority for a review of the certificate.

(2) Subsection (1) is subject to regulations under section 91 (form etc. of applications).

(3) The Secretary of State must by regulations under this section—

(a) require the applicant to give a notice containing details of the application to the club and each responsible authority within such period as may be prescribed;

(b) require the authority to advertise the application and invite representations relating to it to be made to the authority;

(c) prescribe the period during which representations may be made by the club, any responsible authority and any interested party;

(d) require any notice under paragraph (a) or advertisement under paragraph (b) to specify that period.

(4) The relevant licensing authority may, at any time, reject any ground for review specified in an application under this section if it is satisfied—

(a) that the ground is not relevant to one or more of the licensing objectives, or

(b) in the case of an application made by a person other than a responsible authority, that—

(i) the ground is frivolous or vexatious, or

(ii) the ground is a repetition.

(5) For this purpose a ground for review is a repetition if—

(a) it is identical or substantially similar to—

(i) a ground for review specified in an earlier application for review made in respect of the same club premises certificate and determined under section 88, or

(ii) representations considered by the relevant licensing authority in accordance with section 72, before it determined the application for the club premises certificate under that section, and

(b) a reasonable interval has not elapsed since that earlier application or that grant.

(6) Where the authority rejects a ground for review under subsection (4)(b), it must notify the applicant of its decision and, if the ground was rejected because it was frivolous or vexatious, the authority must notify him of its reasons for making that decision.

(7) The application is to be treated as rejected to the extent that any of the grounds for review are rejected under subsection (4).

Accordingly, the requirements imposed under subsection (3)(a) and (b) and by section 88 (so far as not already met) apply only to so much (if any) of the application as has not been rejected.

88 Determination of application for review

(1) This section applies where—

(a) the relevant licensing authority receives an application made in accordance with section 87,

(b) the applicant has complied with any requirement imposed by virtue of subsection (3)(a) or (d) of that section, and

(c) the authority has complied with any requirement imposed on it under subsection (3)(b) or (d) of that section.

(2) Before determining the application, the authority must hold a hearing to consider it and any relevant representations.

(3) The authority must, having regard to the application and any relevant representations, take such of the steps mentioned in subsection (4) (if any) as it considers necessary for the promotion of the licensing objectives.

(4) The steps are—

(a) to modify the conditions of the certificate;

(b) to exclude a qualifying club activity from the scope of the certificate;

(c) to suspend the certificate for a period not exceeding three months;

(d) to withdraw the certificate;

and for this purpose the conditions of the certificate are modified if any of them is altered or omitted or any new condition is added.

(5) Subsection (3) is subject to sections 73 and 74 (mandatory conditions relating to supply of alcohol for consumption off the premises and to exhibition of films).

(6) Where the authority takes a step within subsection (4)(a) or (b), it may provide that the modification or exclusion is to have effect for only such period (not exceeding three months) as it may specify.

(7) In this section "relevant representations" means representations which—

(a) are relevant to one or more of the licensing objectives, and

(b) meet the requirements of subsection (8).

(8) The requirements are—

(a) that the representations are made by the club, a responsible authority or an interested party within the period prescribed under section 87(3)(c),

(b) that they have not been withdrawn, and

(c) if they are made by an interested party (who is not also a responsible authority), that they are not, in the opinion of the relevant licensing authority, frivolous or vexatious.

(9) Where the relevant licensing authority determines that any representations are frivolous or vexatious, it must give the person who made them its reasons for that determination.

(10) Where a licensing authority determines an application for review under this section it must notify the determination and its reasons for making it to—

(a) the club,

(b) the applicant,

(c) any person who made relevant representations, and

(d) the chief officer of police for the police area (or each police area) in which the premises are situated.

(11) A determination under this section does not have effect—

(a) until the end of the period given for appealing against the decision, or

(b) if the decision is appealed against, until the appeal is disposed of.

89 Supplementary provision about review

(1) This section applies where a local authority is both—

(a) the relevant licensing authority, and

(b) a responsible authority,

in respect of any premises.

(2) The authority may, in its capacity as responsible authority, apply under section 87 for a review of any club premises certificate in respect of the premises.

(3) The authority may in its capacity as licensing authority determine that application.

Withdrawal of certificates

90 Club ceasing to be a qualifying club

(1) Where—

(a) a club holds a club premises certificate, and

(b) it appears to the relevant licensing authority that the club does not satisfy the conditions for being a qualifying club in relation to a qualifying club activity to which the certificate relates (see section 61),

the authority must give a notice to the club withdrawing the certificate, so far as relating to that activity.

(2) Where the only reason that the club does not satisfy the conditions for being a qualifying club in relation to the activity in question is that the club has fewer than the required number of members, the notice withdrawing the certificate must state that the withdrawal—

(a) does not take effect until immediately after the end of the period of three months following the date of the notice, and

(b) will not take effect if, at the end of that period, the club again has at least the required number of members.

(3) The references in subsection (2) to the required number of members are references to the minimum number of members required by condition 4 in section 62(5) (25 at the passing of this Act).

(4) Nothing in subsection (2) prevents the giving of a further notice of withdrawal under this section at any time.

(5) Where a justice of the peace is satisfied, on information on oath, that there are reasonable grounds for believing—

(a) that a club which holds a club premises certificate does not satisfy the conditions for being a qualifying club in relation to a qualifying club activity to which the certificate relates, and

(b) that evidence of that fact is to be obtained at the premises to which the certificate relates,

he may issue a warrant authorising a constable to enter the premises, if necessary by force, at any time within one month from the time of the issue of the warrant, and search them.

(6) A person who enters premises under the authority of a warrant under subsection (5) may seize and remove any documents relating to the business of the club in question.

General provision

91 Form etc. of applications and notices under Part 4

In relation to any application or notice under this Part, regulations may prescribe—

(a) its form;

(b) the manner in which it is to be made or given;

(c) information and documents that must accompany it.

92 Fees

(1) Regulations may—

(a) require applications under any provision of this Part (other than section 87) to be accompanied by a fee, and

(b) prescribe the amount of the fee.

(2) Regulations may also require the payment of an annual fee to the relevant licensing authority by or on behalf of a club which holds a club premises certificate.

(3) Regulations under subsection (2) may include provision—

(a) imposing liability for the making of the payment on the secretary or such other officers or members of the club as may be prescribed,

(b) prescribing the amount of any such fee, and

(c) prescribing the time at which any such fee is due.

(4) Any fee which is owed to a licensing authority under subsection (2) may be recovered as a debt due to the authority from any person liable to make the payment by virtue of subsection (3)(a).

Production of certificate, rights of entry, etc.

93 Licensing authority's duty to update club premises certificate

(1) Where—

(a) the relevant licensing authority, in relation to a club premises certificate, makes a determination or receives a notice under this Part, or

(b) an appeal against a decision under this Part is disposed of,

the relevant licensing authority must make the appropriate amendments (if any) to the certificate and, if necessary, issue a new summary of the certificate.

(2) Where a licensing authority is not in possession of the club premises certificate, it may, for the purpose of discharging its obligations under subsection (1), require the secretary of the club to produce the certificate to the authority within 14 days from the date on which the club is notified of the requirement.

(3) A person commits an offence if he fails, without reasonable excuse, to comply with a requirement under subsection (2).

(4) A person guilty of an offence under subsection (3) is liable on summary conviction to a fine not exceeding level 2 on the standard scale.

94 Duty to keep and produce certificate

(1) This section applies whenever premises in respect of which a club premises certificate has effect are being used for one or more qualifying club activities authorised by the certificate.

(2) The secretary of the club must secure that the certificate, or a certified copy of it, is kept at the premises in the custody or under the control of a person (the "nominated person") who—

- (a) falls within subsection (3),
- (b) has been nominated for the purpose by the secretary in writing, and
- (c) has been identified to the relevant licensing authority in a notice given by the secretary.

(3) The persons who fall within this subsection are—

- (a) the secretary of the club,
- (b) any member of the club,
- (c) any person who works at the premises for the purposes of the club.

(4) The nominated person must secure that—

- (a) the summary of the certificate or a certified copy of that summary, and
- (b) a notice specifying the position which he holds at the premises,

are prominently displayed at the premises.

(5) The secretary commits an offence if he fails, without reasonable excuse, to comply with subsection (2).

(6) The nominated person commits an offence if he fails, without reasonable excuse, to comply with subsection (4).

(7) A constable or an authorised person may require the nominated person to produce the club premises certificate (or certified copy) for examination.

(8) An authorised person exercising the power conferred by subsection (7) must, if so requested, produce evidence of his authority to exercise the power.

(9) A person commits an offence if he fails, without reasonable excuse, to produce a club premises certificate or certified copy of a club premises certificate in accordance with a requirement under subsection (7).

(10) A person guilty of an offence under this section is liable on summary conviction to a fine not exceeding level 2 on the standard scale.

(11) In subsection (4) the reference to the summary of the certificate is a reference to the summary issued under section 77 or, where one or more summaries have subsequently been issued under section 93, the most recent summary to be so issued.

(12) Section 95 makes provision about certified copies of club premises certificates and of summaries of club premises certificates for the purposes of this section.

95 Provision supplementary to section 94

(1) Any reference in section 94 to a certified copy of a document is a reference to a copy of the document which is certified to be a true copy by—

- (a) the relevant licensing authority,

(b) a solicitor or notary, or

(c) a person of a prescribed description.

(2) Any certified copy produced in accordance with a requirement under subsection 94(7) must be a copy of the document in the form in which it exists at the time.

(3) A document which purports to be a certified copy of a document is to be taken to be such a copy, and to comply with the requirements of subsection (2), unless the contrary is shown.

96 Inspection of premises before grant of certificate etc.

(1) Subsection (2) applies where—

(a) a club applies for a club premises certificate in respect of any premises,

(b) a club applies under section 84 for the variation of a club premises certificate held by it, or

(c) an application is made under section 87 for review of a club premises certificate.

(2) On production of his authority—

(a) an authorised person, or

(b) a constable authorised by the chief officer of police,

may enter and inspect the premises.

(3) Any entry and inspection under this section must take place at a reasonable time on a day—

(a) which is not more than 14 days after the making of the application in question, and

(b) which is specified in the notice required by subsection (4).

(4) Before an authorised person or constable enters and inspects any premises under this section, at least 48 hours' notice must be given to the club.

(5) Any person obstructing an authorised person in the exercise of the power conferred by this section commits an offence.

(6) A person guilty of an offence under subsection (5) is liable on summary conviction to a fine not exceeding level 2 on the standard scale.

(7) The relevant licensing authority may, on the application of a responsible authority, extend by not more than 7 days the time allowed for carrying out an entry and inspection under this section.

(8) The relevant licensing authority may allow such an extension of time only if it appears to the authority that—

(a) reasonable steps had been taken for an authorised person or constable authorised by the applicant to inspect the premises in good time, but

(b) it was not possible for the inspection to take place within the time allowed.

97 Other powers of entry and search

(1) Where a club premises certificate has effect in respect of any premises, a constable may enter and search the premises if he has reasonable cause to believe—

(a) that an offence under section 4(3)(a), (b) or (c) of the Misuse of Drugs Act 1971 (c. 38) (supplying or offering to supply, or being concerned in supplying or making an offer to supply, a controlled drug) has been, is being, or is about to be, committed there, or

(b) that there is likely to be a breach of the peace there.

(2) A constable exercising any power conferred by this section may, if necessary, use reasonable force.

PART 5

PERMITTED TEMPORARY ACTIVITIES

Introductory

98 Meaning of "permitted temporary activity"

(1) A licensable activity is a permitted temporary activity by virtue of this Part if—

(a) it is carried on in accordance with a notice given in accordance with section 100, and

(b) the following conditions are satisfied.

(2) The first condition is that the requirements of sections 102 (acknowledgement of notice) and 104(1) (notification of police) are met in relation to the notice.

(3) The second condition is that the notice has not been withdrawn under this Part.

(4) The third condition is that no counter notice has been given under this Part in respect of the notice.

99 The relevant licensing authority

In this Part references to the "relevant licensing authority", in relation to any premises, are references to—

(a) the licensing authority in whose area the premises are situated, or

(b) where the premises are situated in the areas of two or more licensing authorities, each of those authorities.

Temporary event notices

100 Temporary event notice

(1) Where it is proposed to use premises for one or more licensable activities during a period not exceeding 96 hours, an individual may give to the relevant licensing authority notice of that proposal (a "temporary event notice").

(2) In this Act, the "premises user", in relation to a temporary event notice, is the individual who gave the notice.

(3) An individual may not give a temporary event notice unless he is aged 18 or over.

(4) A temporary event notice must be in the prescribed form and contain—

(a) a statement of the matters mentioned in subsection (5),

(b) where subsection (6) applies, a statement of the condition mentioned in that subsection, and

(c) such other information as may be prescribed.

(5) Those matters are—

(a) the licensable activities to which the proposal mentioned in subsection (1) relates ("the relevant licensable activities"),

(b) the period (not exceeding 96 hours) during which it is proposed to use the premises for those activities ("the event period"),

(c) the times during the event period when the premises user proposes that those licensable activities shall take place,

(d) the maximum number of persons (being a number less than 500) which the premises user proposes should, during those times, be allowed on the premises at the same time,

(e) where the relevant licensable activities include the supply of alcohol, whether supplies are proposed to be for consumption on the premises or off the premises, or both, and

(f) such other matters as may be prescribed.

(6) Where the relevant licensable activities include the supply of alcohol, the notice must make it a condition of using the premises for such supplies that all such supplies are made by or under the authority of the premises user.

(7) The temporary event notice—

(a) must be given to the relevant licensing authority (in duplicate) no later than ten working days before the day on which the event period begins, and

(b) must be accompanied by the prescribed fee.

(8) The Secretary of State may, by order—

(a) amend subsections (1) and (5)(b) so as to substitute any period for the period for the time being specified there;

(b) amend subsection (5)(d) so as to substitute any number for the number for the time being specified there.

(9) In this section "supply of alcohol" means—

(a) the sale by retail of alcohol, or

(b) the supply of alcohol by or on behalf of a club to, or to the order of, a member of the club.

101 Minimum of 24 hours between event periods

(1) A temporary event notice ("notice A") given by an individual ("the relevant premises user") is void if the event period specified in it does not—

(a) end at least 24 hours before the event period specified in any other temporary event notice given by the relevant premises user in respect of the same premises before or at the same time as notice A, or

(b) begin at least 24 hours after the event period specified in any other such notice.

(2) For the purposes of subsection (1)—

(a) any temporary event notice in respect of which a counter notice has been given under this Part or which has been withdrawn under section 103 is to be disregarded;

(b) a temporary event notice given by an individual who is an associate of the relevant premises user is to be treated as a notice given by the relevant premises user;

(c) a temporary event notice ("notice B") given by an individual who is in business with the relevant premises user is to be treated as a notice given by the relevant premises user if—

(i) that business relates to one or more licensable activities, and

(ii) notice A and notice B relate to one or more licensable activities to which the business relates (although not necessarily the same activity or activities);

(d) two temporary event notices are in respect of the same premises if the whole or any part of the premises in respect of which one of the notices is given includes or forms part of the premises in respect of which the other notice is given.

(3) For the purposes of this section an individual is an associate of another person if that individual is—

(a) the spouse of that person,

(b) a child, parent, grandchild, grandparent, brother or sister of that person,

(c) an agent or employee of that person, or

(d) the spouse of a person within paragraph (b) or (c).

(4) For the purposes of subsection (3) a person living with another as that person's husband or wife is to be treated as that person's spouse.

102 Acknowledgement of notice

(1) Where a licensing authority receives a temporary event notice (in duplicate) in accordance with this Part, it must acknowledge receipt of the notice by sending or delivering one notice to the premises user—

(a) before the end of the first working day following the day on which it was received, or

(b) if the day on which it was received was not a working day, before the end of the second working day following that day.

(2) The authority must mark on the notice to be returned under subsection (1) an acknowledgement of the receipt in the prescribed form.

(3) Subsection (1) does not apply where, before the time by which the notice must be returned in accordance with that subsection, a counter notice has been sent or delivered to the premises user under section 107 in relation to the temporary event notice.

103 Withdrawal of notice

(1) A temporary event notice may be withdrawn by the premises user giving the relevant licensing authority a notice to that effect no later than 24 hours before the beginning of the event period specified in the temporary event notice.

(2) Nothing in section 102 or sections 104 to 107 applies in relation to a notice withdrawn in accordance with this section.

Police objections

104 Objection to notice by the police

(1) The premises user must give a copy of any temporary event notice to the relevant chief officer of police no later than ten working days before the day on which the event period specified in the notice begins.

(2) Where a chief officer of police who receives a copy notice under subsection (1) is satisfied that allowing the premises to be used in accordance with the notice would undermine the crime prevention objective, he must give a notice stating the reasons why he is so satisfied (an "objection notice")—

(a) to the relevant licensing authority, and

(b) to the premises user.

(3) The objection notice must be given no later than 48 hours after the chief officer of police is given a copy of the temporary event notice under subsection (1).

(4) Subsection (2) does not apply at any time after the relevant chief officer of police has received a copy of a counter notice under section 107 in respect of the temporary event notice.

(5) In this section "relevant chief officer of police" means—

(a) where the premises are situated in one police area, the chief officer of police for that area, and

(b) where the premises are situated in two or more police areas, the chief officer of police for each of those areas.

105 Counter notice following police objection

(1) This section applies where an objection notice is given in respect of a temporary event notice.

(2) The relevant licensing authority must—

(a) hold a hearing to consider the objection notice, unless the premises user, the chief officer of police who gave the objection notice and the authority agree that a hearing is unnecessary, and

(b) having regard to the objection notice, give the premises user a counter notice under this section if it considers it necessary for the promotion of the crime prevention objective to do so.

(3) The relevant licensing authority must—

(a) in a case where it decides not to give a counter notice under this section, give the premises user and the relevant chief officer of police notice of the decision, and

(b) in any other case—

(i) give the premises user the counter notice and a notice stating the reasons for its decision, and

(ii) give the relevant chief officer of police a copy of both of those notices.

(4) A decision must be made under subsection (2)(b), and the requirements of subsection (3) must be met, at least 24 hours before the beginning of the event period specified in the temporary event notice.

(5) Where the premises are situated in the area of more than one licensing authority, the functions conferred on the relevant licensing authority by this section must be exercised by those authorities jointly.

(6) This section does not apply—

(a) if the objection notice has been withdrawn (whether by virtue of section 106 or otherwise), or

(b) if the premises user has been given a counter notice under section 107.

(7) In this section "objection notice" and "relevant chief officer of police" have the same meaning as in section 104.

106 Modification of notice following police objection

(1) This section applies where a chief officer of police has given an objection notice in respect of a temporary event notice (and the objection notice has not been withdrawn).

(2) At any time before a hearing is held or dispensed with under section 105(2), the chief officer of police may, with the agreement of the premises user, modify the temporary event notice by making changes to the notice returned to the premises user under section 102.

(3) Where a temporary event notice is modified under subsection (2)—

(a) the objection notice is to be treated for the purposes of this Act as having been withdrawn from the time the temporary event notice is modified, and

(b) from that time—

(i) this Act has effect as if the temporary event notice given under section 100 had been the notice as modified under that subsection, and

(ii) to the extent that the conditions of section 98 are satisfied in relation to the unmodified notice they are to be treated as satisfied in relation to the notice as modified under that subsection.

(4) A copy of the temporary event notice as modified under subsection (2) must be sent or delivered by the chief officer of police to the relevant licensing authority before a hearing is held or dispensed with under section 105(2).

(5) Where the premises are situated in more than one police area, the chief officer of police may modify the temporary event notice under this section only with the consent of the chief officer of police for the other police area or each of the other police areas in which the premises are situated.

(6) This section does not apply if a counter notice has been given under section 107.

(7) In this section "objection notice" has the same meaning as in section 104(2).

Limits on temporary event notices

107 Counter notice where permitted limits exceeded

(1) Where a licensing authority—

(a) receives a temporary event notice ("notice A") in respect of any premises ("the relevant premises"), and

(b) is satisfied that subsection (2), (3), (4) or (5) applies,

the authority must give the premises user ("the relevant premises user") a counter notice under this section.

(2) This subsection applies if the relevant premises user—

(a) holds a personal licence, and

(b) has already given at least 50 temporary event notices in respect of event periods wholly or partly within the same year as the event period specified in notice A.

(3) This subsection applies if the relevant premises user—

(a) does not hold a personal licence, and

(b) has already given at least five temporary event notices in respect of such event periods.

(4) This subsection applies if at least 12 temporary event notices have already been given which—

(a) are in respect of the same premises as notice A, and

(b) specify as the event period a period wholly or partly within the same year as the event period specified in notice A.

(5) This subsection applies if, in any year in which the event period specified in notice A (or any part of it) falls, more than 15 days are days on which one or more of the following fall—

(a) that event period or any part of it,

(b) an event period specified in a temporary event notice already given in respect of the same premises as notice A or any part of such a period.

(6) If the event period in notice A straddles two years, subsections (2), (3) and (4) apply separately in relation to each of those years.

(7) A counter notice under this section must be in the prescribed form and given to the premises user in the prescribed manner.

(8) No such counter notice may be given later than 24 hours before the beginning of the event period specified in notice A.

(9) In determining whether subsection (2), (3), (4) or (5) applies, any temporary event notice in respect of which a counter notice has been given under this section or section 105 is to be disregarded.

(10) In determining for the purposes of subsection (2) or (3) the number of temporary event notices given by the relevant premises user—

(a) a temporary event notice given by an individual who is an associate of the relevant premises user is to be treated as a notice given by the relevant premises user;

(b) a temporary event notice ("notice B") given by an individual who is in business with the relevant premises user is to be treated as a notice given by the relevant premises user if—

(i) that business relates to one or more licensable activities, and

(ii) notice A and notice B relate to one or more licensable activities to which the business relates (but not necessarily the same activity or activities).

(11) Where a licensing authority gives a counter notice under this section it must, forthwith, send a copy of that notice to the chief officer of police for the police area (or each of the police areas) in which the relevant premises are situated.

(12) The Secretary of State may, by order, amend subsection (2)(b), (3)(b), (4) or (5) so as to substitute any number for the number for the time being specified there.

(13) For the purposes of this section—

(a) a temporary event notice is in respect of the same premises as notice A if it is in respect of the whole or any part of the relevant premises or premises which include the whole or any part of those premises,

(b) "year" means calendar year,

(c) "day" means a period of 24 hours beginning at midnight, and

(d) subsections (3) and (4) of section 101 (meaning of "associate") apply as they apply for the purposes of that section.

Rights of entry, production of notice, etc.

108 Right of entry where temporary event notice given

(1) A constable or an authorised officer may, at any reasonable time, enter the premises to which a temporary event notice relates to assess the likely effect of the notice on the promotion of the crime prevention objective.

(2) An authorised officer exercising the power conferred by this section must, if so requested, produce evidence of his authority to exercise the power.

(3) A person commits an offence if he intentionally obstructs an authorised officer exercising a power conferred by this section.

(4) A person guilty of an offence under this section is liable on summary conviction to a fine not exceeding level 2 on the standard scale.

(5) In this section "authorised officer" means—

(a) an officer of the licensing authority in whose area the premises are situated, or

(b) if the premises are situated in the area of more than one licensing authority, an officer of any of those authorities,

authorised for the purposes of this Act.

109 Duty to keep and produce temporary event notice

(1) This section applies whenever premises are being used for one or more licensable activities which are or are purported to be permitted temporary activities by virtue of this Part.

(2) The premises user must either—

(a) secure that a copy of the temporary event notice is prominently displayed at the premises, or

(b) meet the requirements of subsection (3).

(3) The requirements of this subsection are that the premises user must—

(a) secure that the temporary event notice is kept at the premises in—

(i) his custody, or

(ii) in the custody of a person who is present and working at the premises and whom he has nominated for the purposes of this section, and

(b) where the temporary event notice is in the custody of a person so nominated, secure that a notice specifying that fact and the position held at the premises by that person is prominently displayed at the premises.

(4) The premises user commits an offence if he fails, without reasonable excuse, to comply with subsection (2).

(5) Where—

(a) the temporary event notice is not displayed as mentioned in subsection (2)(a), and

(b) no notice is displayed as mentioned in subsection (3)(b),

a constable or authorised officer may require the premises user to produce the temporary event notice for examination.

(6) Where a notice is displayed as mentioned in subsection (3)(b), a constable or authorised officer may require the person specified in that notice to produce the temporary event notice for examination.

(7) An authorised officer exercising the power conferred by subsection (5) or (6) must, if so requested, produce evidence of his authority to exercise the power.

(8) A person commits an offence if he fails, without reasonable excuse, to produce a temporary event notice in accordance with a requirement under subsection (5) or (6).

(9) A person guilty of an offence under this section is liable on summary conviction to a fine not exceeding level 2 on the standard scale.

(10) In this section "authorised officer" has the meaning given in section 108(5).

Miscellaneous

110 Theft, loss, etc. of temporary event notice

(1) Where a temporary event notice acknowledged under section 102 is lost, stolen, damaged or destroyed, the premises user may apply to the licensing authority which acknowledged the notice (or, if there is more than one such authority, any of them) for a copy of the notice.

(2) No application may be made under this section more than one month after the end of the event period specified in the notice.

(3) The application must be accompanied by the prescribed fee.

(4) Where a licensing authority receives an application under this section, it must issue the premises user with a copy of the notice (certified by the authority to be a true copy) if it is satisfied that—

(a) the notice has been lost, stolen, damaged or destroyed, and

(b) where it has been lost or stolen, the premises user has reported that loss or theft to the police.

(5) The copy issued under this section must be a copy of the notice in the form it existed immediately before it was lost, stolen, damaged or destroyed.

(6) This Act applies in relation to a copy issued under this section as it applies in relation to an original notice.

PART 6

PERSONAL LICENCES

Introductory

111 Personal licence

(1) In this Act "personal licence" means a licence which—

(a) is granted by a licensing authority to an individual, and

(b) authorises that individual to supply alcohol, or authorise the supply of alcohol, in accordance with a premises licence.

(2) In subsection (1)(b) the reference to an individual supplying alcohol is to him—

(a) selling alcohol by retail, or

(b) supplying alcohol by or on behalf of a club to, or to the order of, a member of the club.

112 The relevant licensing authority

For the purposes of this Part the "relevant licensing authority", in relation to a personal licence, is the licensing authority which granted the licence.

113 Meaning of "relevant offence" and "foreign offence"

(1) In this Part "relevant offence" means an offence listed in Schedule 4.

(2) The Secretary of State may by order amend that list so as to add, modify or omit any entry.

(3) In this Part "foreign offence" means an offence (other than a relevant offence) under the law of any place outside England and Wales.

114 Spent convictions

For the purposes of this Part a conviction for a relevant offence or a foreign offence must be disregarded if it is spent for the purposes of the Rehabilitation of Offenders Act 1974 (c. 53).

115 Period of validity of personal licence

(1) A personal licence—

(a) has effect for an initial period of ten years beginning with the date on which it is granted, and

(b) may be renewed in accordance with this Part for further periods of ten years at a time.

(2) Subsection (1) is subject to subsections (3) and (4) and to—

(a) section 116 (surrender),

(b) section 119 (continuation of licence pending renewal), and

(c) paragraph 17 of Schedule 5 (continuation of licence pending disposal of appeal).

(3) A personal licence ceases to have effect when it is revoked under section 124 or forfeited under section 129.

(4) And a personal licence does not have effect during any period when it is suspended under section 129.

(5) Subsections (3) and (4) are subject to any court order under sections 129(4) or 130.

116 Surrender of personal licence

(1) Where the holder of a personal licence wishes to surrender his licence he may give the relevant licensing authority a notice to that effect.

(2) The notice must be accompanied by the personal licence or, if that is not practicable, by a statement of the reasons for the failure to provide the licence.

(3) Where a notice of surrender is given in accordance with this section, the personal licence lapses on receipt of the notice by the authority.

Grant and renewal of licences

117 Application for grant or renewal of personal licence

(1) An individual may apply—

(a) for the grant of a personal licence, or

(b) for the renewal of a personal licence held by him.

(2) An application for the grant of a personal licence—

(a) must, if the applicant is ordinarily resident in the area of a licensing authority, be made to that authority, and

(b) may, in any other case, be made to any licensing authority.

(3) An application for the renewal of a personal licence must be made to the relevant licensing authority.

(4) Where the application is for renewal of a personal licence, the application must be accompanied by the personal licence or, if that is not practicable, by a statement of the reasons for the failure to provide the licence.

(5) Subsection (1) is subject to regulations under section 133 (form etc. of applications and notices under this Part).

(6) An application for renewal may be made only during the period of two months beginning three months before the time the licence would expire in accordance with section 115(1) if no application for renewal were made.

118 Individual permitted to hold only one personal licence

(1) An individual who makes an application for the grant of a personal licence under section 117 ("the initial application") may not make another such application until the initial application has been determined by the licensing authority to which it was made or has been withdrawn.

(2) A personal licence is void if, at the time it is granted, the individual to whom it is granted already holds a personal licence.

119 Licence continued pending renewal

(1) Where—

(a) an application for renewal is made in accordance with section 117, and

(b) the application has not been determined before the time the licence would, in the absence of this section, expire,

then, by virtue of this section, the licence continues to have effect for the period beginning with that time and ending with the determination or withdrawal of the application.

(2) Subsection (1) is subject to section 115(3) and (4) (revocation, forfeiture and suspension) and section 116 (surrender).

120 Determination of application for grant

(1) This section applies where an application for the grant of a personal licence is made to a licensing authority in accordance with section 117.

(2) The authority must grant the licence if it appears to it that—

(a) the applicant is aged 18 or over,

(b) he possesses a licensing qualification or is a person of a prescribed description,

(c) no personal licence held by him has been forfeited in the period of five years ending with the day the application was made, and

(d) he has not been convicted of any relevant offence or any foreign offence.

(3) The authority must reject the application if it appears to it that the applicant fails to meet the condition in paragraph (a), (b) or (c) of subsection (2).

(4) If it appears to the authority that the applicant meets the conditions in paragraphs (a), (b) and (c) of that subsection but fails to meet the condition in paragraph (d) of that subsection, the authority must give the chief officer of police for its area a notice to that effect.

(5) Where, having regard to—

(a) any conviction of the applicant for a relevant offence, and

(b) any conviction of his for a foreign offence which the chief officer of police considers to be comparable to a relevant offence,

the chief officer of police is satisfied that granting the licence would undermine the crime prevention objective, he must, within the period of 14 days beginning with the day he received the notice under subsection (4), give the authority a notice stating the reasons why he is so satisfied (an "objection notice").

(6) Where no objection notice is given within that period (or the notice is withdrawn), the authority must grant the application.

(7) In any other case, the authority—

(a) must hold a hearing to consider the objection notice, unless the applicant, the chief officer of police and the authority agree that it is unnecessary, and

(b) having regard to the notice, must—

(i) reject the application if it considers it necessary for the promotion of the crime prevention objective to do so, and

(ii) grant the application in any other case.

(8) In this section "licensing qualification" means—

(a) a qualification—

(i) accredited at the time of its award, and

(ii) awarded by a body accredited at that time,

(b) a qualification awarded before the coming into force of this section which the Secretary of State certifies is to be treated for the purposes of this section as if it were a qualification within paragraph (a), or

(c) a qualification obtained in Scotland or Northern Ireland or in an EEA State (other than the United Kingdom) which is equivalent to a qualification within paragraph (a) or (b).

(9) For this purpose—

"accredited" means accredited by the Secretary of State; and

"EEA State" means a state which is a contracting party to the Agreement on the European Economic Area signed at Oporto on 2nd May 1992, as adjusted by the Protocol signed at Brussels on 17th March 1993.

121 Determination of application for renewal

(1) This section applies where an application for the renewal of a personal licence is made to the relevant licensing authority in accordance with section 117.

(2) If it appears to the authority that the applicant has been convicted of any relevant offence or foreign offence since the relevant time, the relevant licensing authority must give notice to that effect to the chief officer of police for its area.

(3) Where, having regard to—

(a) any conviction of the applicant for a relevant offence, and

(b) any conviction of his for a foreign offence which the chief officer of police considers to be comparable to a relevant offence,

the chief officer of police is satisfied that renewing the licence would undermine the crime prevention objective, he must, within the period of 14 days beginning with the day he received the notice under subsection (2), give the authority a notice stating the reasons why he is so satisfied (an "objection notice").

(4) For the purposes of subsection (3)(a) and (b) it is irrelevant whether the conviction occurred before or after the relevant time.

(5) Where no objection notice is given within that period (or any such notice is withdrawn), the authority must grant the application.

(6) In any other case, the authority—

(a) must hold a hearing to consider the objection notice unless the applicant, the chief officer of police and the authority agree that it is unnecessary, and

(b) having regard to the notice, must—

(i) reject the application if it considers it necessary for the promotion of the crime prevention objective to do so, and

(ii) grant the application in any other case.

(7) In this section "the relevant time" means—

(a) if the personal licence has not been renewed since it was granted, the time it was granted, and

(b) if it has been renewed, the last time it was renewed.

122 Notification of determinations

(1) Where a licensing authority grants an application—

(a) it must give the applicant and the chief officer of police for its area a notice to that effect, and

(b) if the chief officer of police gave an objection notice (which was not withdrawn), the notice under paragraph (a) must contain a statement of the licensing authority's reasons for granting the application.

(2) A licensing authority which rejects an application must give the applicant and the chief officer of police for its area a notice to that effect containing a statement of the authority's reasons for rejecting the application.

(3) In this section—

"application" means an application for the grant or renewal of a personal licence; and

"objection notice" has the meaning given in section 120 or 121, as the case may be.

123 Duty to notify licensing authority of convictions during application period

(1) Where an applicant for the grant or renewal of a personal licence is convicted of a relevant offence or a foreign offence during the application period, he must as soon as reasonably practicable notify the conviction to the authority to which the application is made.

(2) A person commits an offence if he fails, without reasonable excuse, to comply with subsection (1).

(3) A person guilty of an offence under this section is liable on summary conviction to a fine not exceeding level 4 on the standard scale.

(4) In this section "the application period" means the period that—

(a) begins when the application for grant or renewal is made, and

(b) ends when the application is determined or withdrawn.

124 Convictions coming to light after grant or renewal

(1) This section applies where, after a licensing authority has granted or renewed a personal licence, it becomes aware (whether by virtue of section 123(1), 131 or 132 or otherwise) that the holder of a personal licence ("the offender") was convicted during the application period of any relevant offence or foreign offence.

(2) The licensing authority must give a notice to that effect to the chief officer of police for its area.

(3) Where, having regard to—

(a) any conviction of the applicant for a relevant offence, and

(b) any conviction of his for a foreign offence which the chief officer of police considers to be comparable to a relevant offence,

which occurred before the end of the application period, the chief officer of police is satisfied that continuation of the licence would undermine the crime prevention objective, he must, within the period of 14 days beginning with the day he received the notice under subsection (2), give the authority a notice stating the reasons why he is so satisfied (an "objection notice").

(4) Where an objection notice is given within that period (and not withdrawn), the authority—

(a) must hold a hearing to consider the objection notice, unless the holder of the licence, the chief officer of police and the authority agree it is unnecessary, and

(b) having regard to the notice, must revoke the licence if it considers it necessary for the promotion of the crime prevention objective to do so.

(5) Where the authority revokes or decides not to revoke a licence under subsection (4) it must notify the offender and the chief officer of police of the decision and its reasons for making it.

(6) A decision under this section does not have effect—

(a) until the end of the period given for appealing against the decision, or

(b) if the decision is appealed against, until the appeal is disposed of.

(7) In this section "application period", in relation to the grant or renewal of a personal licence, means the period that—

(a) begins when the application for the grant or renewal is made, and

(b) ends at the time of the grant or renewal.

125 Form of personal licence

(1) Where a licensing authority grants a personal licence, it must forthwith issue the applicant with the licence.

(2) The licence must—

(a) specify the holder's name and address, and

(b) identify the licensing authority which granted it.

(3) It must also contain a record of each relevant offence and each foreign offence of which the holder has been convicted, the date of each conviction and the sentence imposed in respect of it.

(4) Subject to subsections (2) and (3), the licence must be in the prescribed form.

126 Theft, loss, etc. of personal licence

(1) Where a personal licence is lost, stolen, damaged or destroyed, the holder of the licence may apply to the relevant licensing authority for a copy of the licence.

(2) Subsection (1) is subject to regulations under section 133(2) (power to prescribe fee to accompany application).

(3) Where the relevant licensing authority receives an application under this section, it must issue the licence holder with a copy of the licence (certified by the authority to be a true copy) if it is satisfied that—

- (a) the licence has been lost, stolen, damaged or destroyed, and
- (b) where it has been lost or stolen, the holder of the licence has reported the loss or theft to the police.

(4) The copy issued under this section must be a copy of the licence in the form in which it existed immediately before it was lost, stolen, damaged or destroyed.

(5) This Act applies in relation to a copy issued under this section as it applies in relation to an original licence.

Duty to notify certain changes

127 Duty to notify change of name or address

(1) The holder of a personal licence must, as soon as reasonably practicable, notify the relevant licensing authority of any change in his name or address as stated in the personal licence.

(2) Subsection (1) is subject to regulations under section 133(2) (power to prescribe fee to accompany notice).

(3) A notice under subsection (1) must also be accompanied by the personal licence or, if that is not practicable, by a statement of the reasons for the failure to provide the licence.

(4) A person commits an offence if he fails, without reasonable excuse, to comply with this section.

(5) A person guilty of an offence under subsection (4) is liable on summary conviction to a fine not exceeding level 2 on the standard scale.

Conviction of licence holder for relevant offence

128 Duty to notify court of personal licence

(1) Where the holder of a personal licence is charged with a relevant offence, he must, no later than the time he makes his first appearance in a magistrates' court in connection with that offence—

(a) produce to the court the personal licence, or

(b) if that is not practicable, notify the court of the existence of the personal licence and the identity of the relevant licensing authority and of the reasons why he cannot produce the licence.

(2) Subsection (3) applies where a person charged with a relevant offence is granted a personal licence—

(a) after his first appearance in a magistrates' court in connection with that offence, but

(b) before—

(i) his conviction, and sentencing for the offence, or his acquittal, or,

(ii) where an appeal is brought against his conviction, sentence or acquittal, the disposal of that appeal.

(3) At his next appearance in court in connection with that offence, that person must—

(a) produce to the court the personal licence, or

(b) if that is not practicable, notify the court of the existence of the personal licence and the identity of the relevant licensing authority and of the reasons why he cannot produce the licence.

(4) Where—

(a) a person charged with a relevant offence has produced his licence to, or notified, a court under subsection (1) or (3), and

(b) before he is convicted of and sentenced for, or acquitted of, that offence, a notifiable event occurs in respect of the licence,

he must, at his next appearance in court in connection with that offence, notify the court of that event.

(5) For this purpose a "notifiable event" in relation to a personal licence means any of the following—

(a) the making or withdrawal of an application for renewal of the licence;

(b) the surrender of the licence under section 116;

(c) the renewal of the licence under section 121;

(d) the revocation of the licence under section 124.

(6) A person commits an offence if he fails, without reasonable excuse, to comply with this section.

(7) A person guilty of an offence under subsection (6) is liable on summary conviction to a fine not exceeding level 2 on the standard scale.

129 Forfeiture or suspension of licence on conviction for relevant offence

(1) This section applies where the holder of a personal licence is convicted of a relevant offence by or before a court in England and Wales.

(2) The court may—

(a) order the forfeiture of the licence, or

(b) order its suspension for a period not exceeding six months.

(3) In determining whether to make an order under subsection (2), the court may take account of any previous conviction of the holder for a relevant offence.

(4) Where a court makes an order under this section it may suspend the order pending an appeal against it.

(5) Subject to subsection (4) and section 130, an order under this section takes effect immediately after it is made.

130 Powers of appellate court to suspend order under section 129

(1) This section applies where—

(a) a person ("the offender") is convicted of a relevant offence, and

(b) an order is made under section 129 in respect of that conviction ("the section 129 order").

(2) In this section any reference to the offender's sentence includes a reference to the section 129 order and to any other order made on his conviction and, accordingly, any reference to an appeal against his sentence includes a reference to an appeal against any order forming part of his sentence.

(3) Where the offender—

(a) appeals to the Crown Court, or

(b) appeals or applies for leave to appeal to the Court of Appeal,

against his conviction or his sentence, the Crown Court or, as the case may be, the Court of Appeal may suspend the section 129 order.

(4) Where the offender appeals or applies for leave to appeal to the House of Lords—

(a) under section 1 of the Administration of Justice Act 1960 (c. 65) from any decision of the High Court which is material to his conviction or sentence, or

(b) under section 33 of the Criminal Appeal Act 1968 (c. 19) from any decision of the Court of Appeal which is material to his conviction or sentence,

the High Court or, as the case may require, the Court of Appeal may suspend the section 129 order.

(5) Where the offender makes an application in respect of the decision of the court in question under section 111 of the Magistrates' Courts Act 1980 (c. 43) (statement of case by magistrates' court) or section 28 of the Supreme Court Act 1981 (c. 54) (statement of case by Crown Court) the High Court may suspend the section 129 order.

(6) Where the offender—

(a) applies to the High Court for a quashing order to remove into the High Court any proceedings of a magistrates' court or of the Crown Court, being proceedings in or in consequence of which he was convicted or his sentence was passed, or

(b) applies to the High Court for permission to make such an application,

the High Court may suspend the section 129 order.

(7) Any power of a court under this section to suspend the section 129 order is a power to do so on such terms as the court thinks fit.

(8) Where, by virtue of this section, a court suspends the section 129 order it must send notice of the suspension to the relevant licensing authority.

(9) Where the section 129 order is an order for forfeiture of the licence, an order under this section to suspend that order has effect to reinstate the licence for the period of the suspension.

131 Court's duty to notify licensing authority of convictions

(1) This section applies where a person who holds a personal licence ("the relevant person") is convicted, by or before a court in England and Wales, of a relevant offence in a case where—

(a) the relevant person has given notice under section 128 (notification of personal licence), or

(b) the court is, for any other reason, aware of the existence of that personal licence.

(2) The appropriate officer of the court must (as soon as reasonably practicable)—

(a) send to the relevant licensing authority a notice specifying—

(i) the name and address of the relevant person,

(ii) the nature and date of the conviction, and

(iii) any sentence passed in respect of it, including any order made under section 129, andsend a copy of the notice to the relevant person.

(3) Where, on an appeal against the relevant person's conviction for the relevant offence or against the sentence imposed on him for that offence, his conviction is quashed or a new sentence is substituted for that sentence, the court which determines the appeal must (as soon as reasonably practicable) arrange—

(a) for notice of the quashing of the conviction or the substituting of the sentence to be sent to the relevant licensing authority, and

(b) for a copy of the notice to be sent to the relevant person.

(4) Where the case is referred to the Court of Appeal under section 36 of the Criminal Justice Act 1988 (c. 33) (review of lenient sentence), the court must cause—

(a) notice of any action it takes under subsection (1) of that section to be sent to the relevant licensing authority, and

(b) a copy of the notice to be sent to the relevant person.

(5) For the purposes of subsection (2) "the appropriate officer" is—

(a) in the case of a magistrates' court, the clerk of the court, and

(b) in the case of the Crown Court, the appropriate officer;

and section 141 of the Magistrates' Courts Act 1980 (c. 43) (meaning of "clerk of a magistrates' court") applies in relation to this subsection as it applies in relation to that section.

132 Licence holder's duty to notify licensing authority of convictions

(1) Subsection (2) applies where the holder of a personal licence—

(a) is convicted of a relevant offence, in a case where section 131(1) does not apply, or

(b) is convicted of a foreign offence.

(2) The holder must—

(a) as soon as reasonably practicable after the conviction, give the relevant licensing authority a notice containing details of the nature and date of the conviction, and any sentence imposed on him in respect of it, and

(b) as soon as reasonably practicable after the determination of any appeal against the conviction or sentence, or of any reference under section 36 of the Criminal Justice Act 1988 (c. 33) in respect of the case, give the relevant licensing authority a notice containing details of the determination.

(3) A notice under subsection (2) must be accompanied by the personal licence or, if that is not practicable, a statement of the reasons for the failure to provide the licence.

(4) A person commits an offence if he fails, without reasonable excuse, to comply with this section.

(5) A person guilty of an offence under subsection (4) is liable on summary conviction to a fine not exceeding level 2 on the standard scale.

General provision

133 Form etc. of applications and notices under Part 6

(1) In relation to any application under section 117 or notice under this Part, regulations may prescribe—

(a) its form,

(b) the manner in which it is to be made or given, and

(c) the information and documents that must accompany it.

(2) Regulations may also—

(a) require applications under section 117 or 126 or notices under section 127 to be accompanied by a fee, and

(b) prescribe the amount of the fee.

134 Licensing authority's duty to update licence document

(1) Where—

(a) the relevant licensing authority makes a determination under section 121 or 124(4),

(b) it receives a notice under section 123(1), 127, 131 or 132, or

(c) an appeal against a decision under this Part is disposed of,

in relation to a personal licence, the authority must make the appropriate amendments (if any) to the licence.

(2) Where, under section 131, notice is given of the making of an order under section 129, the relevant licensing authority must make an endorsement on the licence stating the terms of the order.

(3) Where, under section 131, notice is given of the quashing of such an order, any endorsement previously made under subsection (2) in respect of it must be cancelled.

(4) Where a licensing authority is not in possession of a personal licence, it may, for the purposes of discharging its obligations under this section, require the holder of the licence to produce it to the authority within 14 days beginning with the day on which he is notified of the requirement.

(5) A person commits an offence if he fails, without reasonable excuse, to comply with a requirement under subsection (4).

(6) A person guilty of an offence under subsection (5) is liable on summary conviction to a fine not exceeding level 2 on the standard scale.

Production of licence

135 Licence holder's duty to produce licence

(1) This section applies where the holder of a personal licence is on premises to make or authorise the supply of alcohol, and such supplies—

- (a) are authorised by a premises licence in respect of those premises, or
- (b) are a permitted temporary activity on the premises by virtue of a temporary event notice given under Part 5 in respect of which he is the premises user.

(2) Any constable or authorised officer may require the holder of the personal licence to produce that licence for examination.

(3) An authorised officer exercising the power conferred by subsection (2) must, if so requested, produce evidence of his authority to exercise the power.

(4) A person who fails, without reasonable excuse, to comply with a requirement under subsection (2) is guilty of an offence.

(5) A person guilty of an offence under subsection (4) is liable on summary conviction to a fine not exceeding level 2 on the standard scale.

(6) In this section "authorised officer" means an officer of a licensing authority authorised by the authority for the purposes of this Act.

PART 7

OFFENCES

Unauthorised licensable activities

136 Unauthorised licensable activities

(1) A person commits an offence if—

- (a) he carries on or attempts to carry on a licensable activity on or from any premises otherwise than under and in accordance with an authorisation, or
- (b) he knowingly allows a licensable activity to be so carried on.

(2) Where the licensable activity in question is the provision of regulated entertainment, a person does not commit an offence under this section if his only involvement in the provision of the entertainment is that he—

(a) performs in a play,

(b) participates as a sportsman in an indoor sporting event,

(c) boxes or wrestles in a boxing or wrestling entertainment,

(d) performs live music,

(e) plays recorded music,

(f) performs dance, or

(g) does something coming within paragraph 2(1)(h) of Schedule 1 (entertainment similar to music, dance, etc.).

(3) Subsection (2) is to be construed in accordance with Part 3 of Schedule 1.

(4) A person guilty of an offence under this section is liable on summary conviction to imprisonment for a term not exceeding six months or to a fine not exceeding £20,000, or to both.

(5) In this Part "authorisation" means—

(a) a premises licence,

(b) a club premises certificate, or

(c) a temporary event notice in respect of which the conditions of section 98(2) to (4) are satisfied.

137 Exposing alcohol for unauthorised sale

(1) A person commits an offence if, on any premises, he exposes for sale by retail any alcohol in circumstances where the sale by retail of that alcohol on those premises would be an unauthorised licensable activity.

(2) For that purpose a licensable activity is unauthorised unless it is under and in accordance with an authorisation.

(3) A person guilty of an offence under this section is liable on summary conviction to imprisonment for a term not exceeding six months or to a fine not exceeding £20,000, or to both.

(4) The court by which a person is convicted of an offence under this section may order the alcohol in question, and any container for it, to be forfeited and either destroyed or dealt with in such other manner as the court may order.

138 Keeping alcohol on premises for unauthorised sale etc.

(1) A person commits an offence if he has in his possession or under his control alcohol which he intends to sell by retail or supply in circumstances where that activity would be an unauthorised licensable activity.

(2) For that purpose a licensable activity is unauthorised unless it is under and in accordance with an authorisation.

(3) In subsection (1) the reference to the supply of alcohol is a reference to the supply of alcohol by or on behalf of a club to, or to the order of, a member of the club.

(4) A person guilty of an offence under this section is liable on summary conviction to a fine not exceeding level 2 on the standard scale.

(5) The court by which a person is convicted of an offence under this section may order the alcohol in question, and any container for it, to be forfeited and either destroyed or dealt with in such other manner as the court may order.

139 Defence of due diligence

(1) In proceedings against a person for an offence to which subsection (2) applies, it is a defence that—

- (a) his act was due to a mistake, or to reliance on information given to him, or to an act or omission by another person, or to some other cause beyond his control, and
- (b) he took all reasonable precautions and exercised all due diligence to avoid committing the offence.

(2) This subsection applies to an offence under—

- (a) section 136(1)(a) (carrying on unauthorised licensable activity),
- (b) section 137 (exposing alcohol for unauthorised sale), or
- (c) section 138 (keeping alcohol on premises for unauthorised sale).

Drunkenness and disorderly conduct

140 Allowing disorderly conduct on licensed premises etc.

(1) A person to whom subsection (2) applies commits an offence if he knowingly allows disorderly conduct on relevant premises.

(2) This subsection applies—

- (a) to any person who works at the premises in a capacity, whether paid or unpaid, which authorises him to prevent the conduct,
- (b) in the case of licensed premises, to—
  - (i) the holder of a premises licence in respect of the premises, and
  - (ii) the designated premises supervisor (if any) under such a licence,
- (c) in the case of premises in respect of which a club premises certificate has effect, to any member or officer of the club which holds the certificate who at the time the conduct takes place is present on the premises in a capacity which enables him to prevent it, and
- (d) in the case of premises which may be used for a permitted temporary activity by virtue of Part 5, to the premises user in relation to the temporary event notice in question.

(3) A person guilty of an offence under this section is liable on summary conviction to a fine not exceeding level 3 on the standard scale.

141 Sale of alcohol to a person who is drunk

(1) A person to whom subsection (2) applies commits an offence if, on relevant premises, he knowingly—

(a) sells or attempts to sell alcohol to a person who is drunk, or
(b) allows alcohol to be sold to such a person.

(2) This subsection applies—
(a) to any person who works at the premises in a capacity, whether paid or unpaid, which gives him authority to sell the alcohol concerned,
(b) in the case of licensed premises, to—
(i) the holder of a premises licence in respect of the premises, and
(ii) the designated premises supervisor (if any) under such a licence,
(c) in the case of premises in respect of which a club premises certificate has effect, to any member or officer of the club which holds the certificate who at the time the sale (or attempted sale) takes place is present on the premises in a capacity which enables him to prevent it, and
(d) in the case of premises which may be used for a permitted temporary activity by virtue of Part 5, to the premises user in relation to the temporary event notice in question.

(3) This section applies in relation to the supply of alcohol by or on behalf of a club to or to the order of a member of the club as it applies in relation to the sale of alcohol.

(4) A person guilty of an offence under this section is liable on summary conviction to a fine not exceeding level 3 on the standard scale.

142 Obtaining alcohol for a person who is drunk

(1) A person commits an offence if, on relevant premises, he knowingly obtains or attempts to obtain alcohol for consumption on those premises by a person who is drunk.

(2) A person guilty of an offence under this section is liable on summary conviction to a fine not exceeding level 3 on the standard scale.

143 Failure to leave licensed premises etc.

(1) A person who is drunk or disorderly commits an offence if, without reasonable excuse—
(a) he fails to leave relevant premises when requested to do so by a constable or by a person to whom subsection (2) applies, or
(b) he enters or attempts to enter relevant premises after a constable or a person to whom subsection (2) applies has requested him not to enter.

(2) This subsection applies—
(a) to any person who works at the premises in a capacity, whether paid or unpaid, which authorises him to make such a request,
(b) in the case of licensed premises, to—
(i) the holder of a premises licence in respect of the premises, or
(ii) the designated premises supervisor (if any) under such a licence,
(c) in the case of premises in respect of which a club premises certificate has effect, to any member or officer of the club which holds the certificate who is present on the premises in a capacity which enables him to make such a request, and

(d) in the case of premises which may be used for a permitted temporary activity by virtue of Part 5, to the premises user in relation to the temporary event notice in question.

(3) A person guilty of an offence under subsection (1) is liable on summary conviction to a fine not exceeding level 1 on the standard scale.

(4) On being requested to do so by a person to whom subsection (2) applies, a constable must—

(a) help to expel from relevant premises a person who is drunk or disorderly;

(b) help to prevent such a person from entering relevant premises.

Smuggled goods

144 Keeping of smuggled goods

(1) A person to whom subsection (2) applies commits an offence if he knowingly keeps or allows to be kept, on any relevant premises, any goods which have been imported without payment of duty or which have otherwise been unlawfully imported.

(2) This subsection applies—

(a) to any person who works at the premises in a capacity, whether paid or unpaid, which gives him authority to prevent the keeping of the goods on the premises,

(b) in the case of licensed premises, to—

(i) the holder of a premises licence in respect of the premises, and

(ii) the designated premises supervisor (if any) under such a licence,

(c) in the case of premises in respect of which a club premises certificate has effect, to any member or officer of the club which holds the certificate who is present on the premises at any time when the goods are kept on the premises in a capacity which enables him to prevent them being so kept, and

(d) in the case of premises which may be used for a permitted temporary activity by virtue of Part 5, to the premises user in relation to the temporary event notice in question.

(3) A person guilty of an offence under this section is liable on summary conviction to a fine not exceeding level 3 on the standard scale.

(4) The court by which a person is convicted of an offence under this section may order the goods in question, and any container for them, to be forfeited and either destroyed or dealt with in such other manner as the court may order.

Children and alcohol

145 Unaccompanied children prohibited from certain premises

(1) A person to whom subsection (3) applies commits an offence if—

(a) knowing that relevant premises are within subsection (4), he allows an unaccompanied child to be on the premises at a time when they are open for the purposes of being used for the supply of alcohol for consumption there, or

(b) he allows an unaccompanied child to be on relevant premises at a time between the hours of midnight and 5 a.m. when the premises are open for the purposes of being used for the supply of alcohol for consumption there.

(2) For the purposes of this section—

(a) "child" means an individual aged under 16,

(b) a child is unaccompanied if he is not in the company of an individual aged 18 or over.

(3) This subsection applies—

(a) to any person who works at the premises in a capacity, whether paid or unpaid, which authorises him to request the unaccompanied child to leave the premises,

(b) in the case of licensed premises, to—

(i) the holder of a premises licence in respect of the premises, and

(ii) the designated premises supervisor (if any) under such a licence,

(c) in the case of premises in respect of which a club premises certificate has effect, to any member or officer of the club which holds the certificate who is present on the premises in a capacity which enables him to make such a request, and

(d) in the case of premises which may be used for a permitted temporary activity by virtue of Part 5, to the premises user in relation to the temporary event notice in question.

(4) Relevant premises are within this subsection if—

(a) they are exclusively or primarily used for the supply of alcohol for consumption on the premises, or

(b) they are open for the purposes of being used for the supply of alcohol for consumption on the premises by virtue of Part 5 (permitted temporary activities) and, at the time the temporary event notice in question has effect, they are exclusively or primarily used for such supplies.

(5) No offence is committed under this section if the unaccompanied child is on the premises solely for the purpose of passing to or from some other place to or from which there is no other convenient means of access or egress.

(6) Where a person is charged with an offence under this section by reason of his own conduct it is a defence that—

(a) he believed that the unaccompanied child was aged 16 or over or that an individual accompanying him was aged 18 or over, and

(b) either—

(i) he had taken all reasonable steps to establish the individual's age, or

(ii) nobody could reasonably have suspected from the individual's appearance that he was aged under 16 or, as the case may be, under 18.

(7) For the purposes of subsection (6), a person is treated as having taken all reasonable steps to establish an individual's age if—

(a) he asked the individual for evidence of his age, and

(b) the evidence would have convinced a reasonable person.

(8) Where a person ("the accused") is charged with an offence under this section by reason of the act or default of some other person, it is a defence that the accused exercised all due diligence to avoid committing it.

(9) A person guilty of an offence under this section is liable on summary conviction to a fine not exceeding level 3 on the standard scale.

(10) In this section "supply of alcohol" means—

(a) the sale by retail of alcohol, or

(b) the supply of alcohol by or on behalf of a club to, or to the order of, a member of the club.

146 Sale of alcohol to children

(1) A person commits an offence if he sells alcohol to an individual aged under 18.

(2) A club commits an offence if alcohol is supplied by it or on its behalf—

(a) to, or to the order of, a member of the club who is aged under 18, or

(b) to the order of a member of the club, to an individual who is aged under 18.

(3) A person commits an offence if he supplies alcohol on behalf of a club—

(a) to, or to the order of, a member of the club who is aged under 18, or

(b) to the order of a member of the club, to an individual who is aged under 18.

(4) Where a person is charged with an offence under this section by reason of his own conduct it is a defence that—

(a) he believed that the individual was aged 18 or over, and

(b) either—

(i) he had taken all reasonable steps to establish the individual's age, or

(ii) nobody could reasonably have suspected from the individual's appearance that he was aged under 18.

(5) For the purposes of subsection (4), a person is treated as having taken all reasonable steps to establish an individual's age if—

(a) he asked the individual for evidence of his age, and

(b) the evidence would have convinced a reasonable person.

(6) Where a person ("the accused") is charged with an offence under this section by reason of the act or default of some other person, it is a defence that the accused exercised all due diligence to avoid committing it.

(7) A person guilty of an offence under this section is liable on summary conviction to a fine not exceeding level 5 on the standard scale.

147 Allowing the sale of alcohol to children

(1) A person to whom subsection (2) applies commits an offence if he knowingly allows the sale of alcohol on relevant premises to an individual aged under 18.

(2) This subsection applies to a person who works at the premises in a capacity, whether paid or unpaid, which authorises him to prevent the sale.

(3) A person to whom subsection (4) applies commits an offence if he knowingly allows alcohol to be supplied on relevant premises by or on behalf of a club—

(a) to or to the order of a member of the club who is aged under 18, or

(b) to the order of a member of the club, to an individual who is aged under 18.

(4) This subsection applies to—

(a) a person who works on the premises in a capacity, whether paid or unpaid, which authorises him to prevent the supply, and

(b) any member or officer of the club who at the time of the supply is present on the relevant premises in a capacity which enables him to prevent it.

(5) A person guilty of an offence under this section is liable on summary conviction to a fine not exceeding level 5 on the standard scale.

148 Sale of liqueur confectionery to children under 16

(1) A person commits an offence if he—

(a) sells liqueur confectionery to an individual aged under 16, or

(b) supplies such confectionery, on behalf of a club—

(i) to or to the order of a member of the club who is aged under 16, or

(ii) to the order of a member of the club, to an individual who is aged under 16.

(2) A club commits an offence if liqueur confectionery is supplied by it or on its behalf—

(a) to or to the order of a member of the club who is aged under 16, or

(b) to the order of a member of the club, to an individual who is aged under 16.

(3) Where a person is charged with an offence under this section by reason of his own conduct it is a defence that—

(a) he believed that the individual was aged 16 or over, and

(b) either—

(i) he had taken all reasonable steps to establish the individual's age, or

(ii) nobody could reasonably have suspected from the individual's appearance that he was aged under 16.

(4) For the purposes of subsection (3), a person is treated as having taken all reasonable steps to establish an individual's age if—

(a) he asked the individual for evidence of his age, and

(b) the evidence would have convinced a reasonable person.

(5) Where a person ("the accused") is charged with an offence under this section by reason of the act or default of some other person, it is a defence that the accused exercised all due diligence to avoid committing it.

(6) A person guilty of an offence under this section is liable on summary conviction to a fine not exceeding level 2 on the standard scale.

(7) In this section "liqueur confectionery" has the meaning given in section 191(2).

149 Purchase of alcohol by or on behalf of children

(1) An individual aged under 18 commits an offence if—

(a) he buys or attempts to buy alcohol, or

(b) where he is a member of a club—

(i) alcohol is supplied to him or to his order by or on behalf of the club, as a result of some act or default of his, or

(ii) he attempts to have alcohol supplied to him or to his order by or on behalf of the club.

(2) But subsection (1) does not apply where the individual buys or attempts to buy the alcohol at the request of—

(a) a constable, or

(b) a weights and measures inspector,

who is acting in the course of his duty.

(3) A person commits an offence if—

(a) he buys or attempts to buy alcohol on behalf of an individual aged under 18, or

(b) where he is a member of a club, on behalf of an individual aged under 18 he—

(i) makes arrangements whereby alcohol is supplied to him or to his order by or on behalf of the club, or

(ii) attempts to make such arrangements.

(4) A person ("the relevant person") commits an offence if—

(a) he buys or attempts to buy alcohol for consumption on relevant premises by an individual aged under 18, or

(b) where he is a member of a club—

(i) by some act or default of his, alcohol is supplied to him, or to his order, by or on behalf of the club for consumption on relevant premises by an individual aged under 18, or

(ii) he attempts to have alcohol so supplied for such consumption.

(5) But subsection (4) does not apply where—

(a) the relevant person is aged 18 or over,

(b) the individual is aged 16 or 17,

(c) the alcohol is beer, wine or cider,

(d) its purchase or supply is for consumption at a table meal on relevant premises, and

(e) the individual is accompanied at the meal by an individual aged 18 or over.

(6) Where a person is charged with an offence under subsection (3) or (4) it is a defence that he had no reason to suspect that the individual was aged under 18.

(7) A person guilty of an offence under this section is liable on summary conviction—

(a) in the case of an offence under subsection (1), to a fine not exceeding level 3 on the standard scale, and

(b) in the case of an offence under subsection (3) or (4), to a fine not exceeding level 5 on the standard scale.

150 Consumption of alcohol by children

(1) An individual aged under 18 commits an offence if he knowingly consumes alcohol on relevant premises.

(2) A person to whom subsection (3) applies commits an offence if he knowingly allows the consumption of alcohol on relevant premises by an individual aged under 18.

(3) This subsection applies—

(a) to a person who works at the premises in a capacity, whether paid or unpaid, which authorises him to prevent the consumption, and

(b) where the alcohol was supplied by a club to or to the order of a member of the club, to any member or officer of the club who is present at the premises at the time of the consumption in a capacity which enables him to prevent it.

(4) Subsections (1) and (2) do not apply where—

(a) the individual is aged 16 or 17,

(b) the alcohol is beer, wine or cider,

(c) its consumption is at a table meal on relevant premises, and

(d) the individual is accompanied at the meal by an individual aged 18 or over.

(5) A person guilty of an offence under this section is liable on summary conviction—

(a) in the case of an offence under subsection (1), to a fine not exceeding level 3 on the standard scale, and

(b) in the case of an offence under subsection (2), to a fine not exceeding level 5 on the standard scale.

151 Delivering alcohol to children

(1) A person who works on relevant premises in any capacity, whether paid or unpaid, commits an offence if he knowingly delivers to an individual aged under 18—

(a) alcohol sold on the premises, or

(b) alcohol supplied on the premises by or on behalf of a club to or to the order of a member of the club.

(2) A person to whom subsection (3) applies commits an offence if he knowingly allows anybody else to deliver to an individual aged under 18 alcohol sold on relevant premises.

(3) This subsection applies to a person who works on the premises in a capacity, whether paid or unpaid, which authorises him to prevent the delivery of the alcohol.

(4) A person to whom subsection (5) applies commits an offence if he knowingly allows anybody else to deliver to an individual aged under 18 alcohol supplied on relevant premises by or on behalf of a club to or to the order of a member of the club.

(5) This subsection applies—

(a) to a person who works on the premises in a capacity, whether paid or unpaid, which authorises him to prevent the supply, and

(b) to any member or officer of the club who at the time of the supply in question is present on the premises in a capacity which enables him to prevent the supply.

(6) Subsections (1), (2) and (4) do not apply where—

(a) the alcohol is delivered at a place where the buyer or, as the case may be, person supplied lives or works, or

(b) the individual aged under 18 works on the relevant premises in a capacity, whether paid or unpaid, which involves the delivery of alcohol, or

(c) the alcohol is sold or supplied for consumption on the relevant premises.

(7) A person guilty of an offence under this section is liable on summary conviction to a fine not exceeding level 5 on the standard scale.

152 Sending a child to obtain alcohol

(1) A person commits an offence if he knowingly sends an individual aged under 18 to obtain—

(a) alcohol sold or to be sold on relevant premises for consumption off the premises, or

(b) alcohol supplied or to be supplied by or on behalf of a club to or to the order of a member of the club for such consumption.

(2) For the purposes of this section, it is immaterial whether the individual aged under 18 is sent to obtain the alcohol from the relevant premises or from other premises from which it is delivered in pursuance of the sale or supply.

(3) Subsection (1) does not apply where the individual aged under 18 works on the relevant premises in a capacity, whether paid or unpaid, which involves the delivery of alcohol.

(4) Subsection (1) also does not apply where the individual aged under 18 is sent by—

(a) a constable, or

(b) a weights and measures inspector,

who is acting in the course of his duty.

(5) A person guilty of an offence under this section is liable on summary conviction to a fine not exceeding level 5 on the standard scale.

153 Prohibition of unsupervised sales by children

(1) A responsible person commits an offence if on any relevant premises he knowingly allows an individual aged under 18 to make on the premises—

(a) any sale of alcohol, or

(b) any supply of alcohol by or on behalf of a club to or to the order of a member of the club,

unless the sale or supply has been specifically approved by that or another responsible person.

(2) But subsection (1) does not apply where—

(a) the alcohol is sold or supplied for consumption with a table meal,

(b) it is sold or supplied in premises which are being used for the service of table meals (or in a part of any premises which is being so used), and

(c) the premises are (or the part is) not used for the sale or supply of alcohol otherwise than to persons having table meals there and for consumption by such a person as an ancillary to his meal.

(3) A person guilty of an offence under this section is liable on summary conviction to a fine not exceeding level 1 on the standard scale.

(4) In this section “responsible person” means—

(a) in relation to licensed premises—

(i) the holder of a premises licence in respect of the premises,

(ii) the designated premises supervisor (if any) under such a licence, or

(iii) any individual aged 18 or over who is authorised for the purposes of this section by such a holder or supervisor,

(b) in relation to premises in respect of which there is in force a club premises certificate, any member or officer of the club present on the premises in a capacity which enables him to prevent the supply in question, and

(c) in relation to premises which may be used for a permitted temporary activity by virtue of Part 5—

(i) the premises user, or

(ii) any individual aged 18 or over who is authorised for the purposes of this section by the premises user.

154 Enforcement role for weights and measures authorities

(1) It is the duty of every local weights and measures authority in England and Wales to enforce within its area the provisions of sections 146 and 147, so far as they apply to sales of alcohol made on or from premises to which the public have access.

(2) A weights and measures inspector may make, or authorise any person to make on his behalf, such purchases of goods as appear expedient for the purpose of determining whether those provisions are being complied with.

Confiscation of alcohol

155 Confiscation of sealed containers of alcohol

(1) In section 1 of the Confiscation of Alcohol (Young Persons) Act 1997 (c. 33) (right to require surrender of alcohol)—

(a) in subsection (1), omit "(other than a sealed container)",

(b) after that subsection insert—

"(1A) But a constable may not under subsection (1) require a person to surrender any sealed container unless the constable reasonably believes that the person is, or has been, consuming, or intends to consume, alcohol in any relevant place., and"

(c) in subsection (6), after "subsection (1)" insert "and (1A)".

(2) In section 12(2)(b) of the Criminal Justice and Police Act 2001 (c. 16) (right to require surrender of alcohol), omit "(other than a sealed container)".

Vehicles and trains

156 Prohibition on sale of alcohol on moving vehicles

(1) A person commits an offence under this section if he sells by retail alcohol on or from a vehicle at a time when the vehicle is not permanently or temporarily parked.

(2) A person guilty of an offence under this section is liable on summary conviction to imprisonment for a term not exceeding three months or to a fine not exceeding £20,000, or to both.

(3) In proceedings against a person for an offence under this section, it is a defence that—

(a) his act was due to a mistake, or to reliance on information given to him, or to an act or omission by another person, or to some other cause beyond his control, and

(b) he took all reasonable precautions and exercised all due diligence to avoid committing the offence.

157 Power to prohibit sale of alcohol on trains

(1) A magistrates' court acting for a petty sessions area may make an order prohibiting the sale of alcohol, during such period as may be specified, on any railway vehicle—

(a) at such station or stations as may be specified, being stations in that area, or

(b) travelling between such stations as may be specified, at least one of which is in that area.

(2) A magistrates' court may make an order under this section only on the application of a senior police officer.

(3) A magistrates' court may not make such an order unless it is satisfied that the order is necessary to prevent disorder.

(4) Where an order is made under this section, the responsible senior police officer must, forthwith, serve a copy of the order on the train operator (or each train operator) affected by the order.

(5) A person commits an offence if he knowingly—

(a) sells or attempts to sell alcohol in contravention of an order under this section, or

(b) allows the sale of alcohol in contravention of such an order.

(6) A person guilty of an offence under this section is liable on summary conviction to imprisonment for a term not exceeding three months or to a fine not exceeding £20,000, or to both.

(7) In this section—

"railway vehicle" has the meaning given by section 83 of the Railways Act 1993;

"responsible senior police officer", in relation to an order under this section, means the senior police officer who applied for the order or, if the chief officer of police of the force in question has designated another senior police officer for the purpose, that other officer;

"senior police officer" means a police officer of, or above, the rank of inspector;

"specified" means specified in the order under this section;

"station" has the meaning given by section 83 of the Railways Act 1993 (c. 43); and

"train operator" means a person authorised by a licence under section 8 of that Act to operate railway assets (within the meaning of section 6 of that Act).

False statement relating to licensing etc.

158 False statements made for the purposes of this Act

(1) A person commits an offence if he knowingly or recklessly makes a false statement in or in connection with—

(a) an application for the grant, variation, transfer or review of a premises licence or club premises certificate,

(b) an application for a provisional statement,

(c) a temporary event notice, an interim authority notice or any other notice under this Act,

(d) an application for the grant or renewal of a personal licence, or

(e) a notice within section 178(1) (notice by freeholder etc. conferring right to be notified of changes to licensing register).

(2) For the purposes of subsection (1) a person is to be treated as making a false statement if he produces, furnishes, signs or otherwise makes use of a document that contains a false statement.

(3) A person guilty of an offence under this section is liable on summary conviction to a fine not exceeding level 5 on the standard scale.

Interpretation

159 Interpretation of Part 7

In this Part—

"authorisation" has the meaning given in section 136(5);

"relevant premises" means—

(a) licensed premises, or

(b) premises in respect of which there is in force a club premises certificate, or

(c) premises which may be used for a permitted temporary activity by virtue of Part 5;

"table meal" means a meal eaten by a person seated at a table, or at a counter or other structure which serves the purpose of a table and is not used for the service of refreshments for consumption by persons not seated at a table or structure serving the purpose of a table; and

"weights and measures inspector" means an inspector of weights and measures appointed under section 72(1) of the Weights and Measures Act 1985 (c. 72).

PART 8

CLOSURE OF PREMISES

Closure of premises in an identified area

160 Orders to close premises in area experiencing disorder

(1) Where there is or is expected to be disorder in any petty sessions area, a magistrates' court acting for the area may make an order requiring all premises—

(a) which are situated at or near the place of the disorder or expected disorder, and

(b) in respect of which a premises licence or a temporary event notice has effect,

to be closed for a period, not exceeding 24 hours, specified in the order.

(2) A magistrates' court may make an order under this section only on the application of a police officer who is of the rank of superintendent or above.

(3) A magistrates' court may not make such an order unless it is satisfied that it is necessary to prevent disorder.

(4) Where an order is made under this section, a person to whom subsection (5) applies commits an offence if he knowingly keeps any premises to which the order relates open, or allows any such premises to be kept open, during the period of the order.

(5) This subsection applies—

(a) to any manager of the premises,

(b) in the case of licensed premises, to—

(i) the holder of a premises licence in respect of the premises, and

(ii) the designated premises supervisor (if any) under such a licence, and

(c) in the case of premises in respect of which a temporary event notice has effect, to the premises user in relation to that notice.

(6) A person guilty of an offence under subsection (4) is liable on summary conviction to a fine not exceeding level 3 on the standard scale.

(7) A constable may use such force as may be necessary for the purpose of closing premises ordered to be closed under this section.

Closure of identified premises

161 Closure orders for identified premises

(1) A senior police officer may make a closure order in relation to any relevant premises if he reasonably believes that—

(a) there is, or is likely imminently to be, disorder on, or in the vicinity of and related to, the premises and their closure is necessary in the interests of public safety, or

(b) a public nuisance is being caused by noise coming from the premises and the closure of the premises is necessary to prevent that nuisance.

(2) A closure order is an order under this section requiring relevant premises to be closed for a period not exceeding 24 hours beginning with the coming into force of the order.

(3) In determining whether to make a closure order in respect of any premises, the senior police officer must have regard, in particular, to the conduct of each appropriate person in relation to the disorder or nuisance.

(4) A closure order must—

(a) specify the premises to which it relates,

(b) specify the period for which the premises are to be closed,

(c) specify the grounds on which it is made, and

(d) state the effect of sections 162 to 168.

(5) A closure order in respect of any relevant premises comes into force at the time a constable gives notice of it to an appropriate person who is connected with any of the activities to which the disorder or nuisance relates.

(6) A person commits an offence if, without reasonable excuse, he permits relevant premises to be open in contravention of a closure order or any extension of it.

(7) A person guilty of an offence under subsection (6) is liable on summary conviction to imprisonment for a term not exceeding three months or to a fine not exceeding £20,000, or to both.

(8) In this section—

"relevant premises" means premises in respect of which one or more of the following have effect—

(a) a premises licence,

(b) a temporary event notice; and

"senior police officer" means a police officer of, or above, the rank of inspector.

162 Extension of closure order

(1) Where, before the end of the period for which relevant premises are to be closed under a closure order or any extension of it (the "closure period"), the responsible senior police officer reasonably believes that—

(a) a relevant magistrates' court will not have determined whether to exercise its powers under section 165(2) in respect of the closure order, and any extension of it, by the end of the closure period, and

(b) the conditions for an extension are satisfied,

he may extend the closure period for a further period not exceeding 24 hours beginning with the end of the previous closure period.

(2) The conditions for an extension are that—

(a) in the case of an order made by virtue of section 161(1)(a), closure is necessary in the interests of public safety because of disorder or likely disorder on, or in the vicinity of and related to, the premises,

(b) in the case of an order made by virtue of section 161(1)(b), closure is necessary to ensure that no public nuisance is, or is likely to be, caused by noise coming from the premises.

(3) An extension in relation to any relevant premises comes into force when a constable gives notice of it to an appropriate person connected with any of the activities to which the disorder or nuisance relates or is expected to relate.

(4) But the extension does not come into force unless the notice is given before the end of the previous closure period.

163 Cancellation of closure order

(1) The responsible senior police officer may cancel a closure order and any extension of it at any time—

(a) after the making of the order, but

(b) before a relevant magistrates' court has determined whether to exercise its powers under section 165(2) in respect of the order and any extension of it.

(2) The responsible senior police officer must cancel a closure order and any extension of it if he does not reasonably believe that—

(a) in the case of an order made by virtue of section 161(1)(a), closure is necessary in the interests of public safety because of disorder or likely disorder on, or in the vicinity of and related to, the premises,

(b) in the case of an order made by virtue of section 161(1)(b), closure is necessary to ensure that no public nuisance is, or is likely to be, caused by noise coming from the premises.

(3) Where a closure order and any extension of it are cancelled under this section, the responsible senior police officer must give notice of the cancellation to an appropriate person connected with any of the activities related to the disorder (or anticipated disorder) or nuisance in respect of which the closure order was made.

164 Application to magistrates' court by police

(1) The responsible senior police officer must, as soon as reasonably practicable after a closure order comes into force in respect of any relevant premises, apply to a relevant magistrates court for it to consider the order and any extension of it.

(2) Where an application is made under this section in respect of licensed premises, the responsible senior officer must also notify the relevant licensing authority—

(a) that a closure order has come into force,

(b) of the contents of the order and of any extension of it, and

(c) of the application under subsection (1).

165 Consideration of closure order by magistrates' court

(1) A relevant magistrates' court must as soon as reasonably practicable after receiving an application under section 164(1)—

(a) hold a hearing to consider whether it is appropriate to exercise any of the court's powers under subsection (2) in relation to the closure order or any extension of it, and

(b) determine whether to exercise any of those powers.

(2) The relevant magistrates' court may—

(a) revoke the closure order and any extension of it;

(b) order the premises to remain, or to be, closed until such time as the relevant licensing authority has made a determination in respect of the order for the purposes of section 167;

(c) order the premises to remain or to be closed until that time subject to such exceptions as may be specified in the order;

(d) order the premises to remain or to be closed until that time unless such conditions as may be specified in the order are satisfied.

(3) In determining whether the premises will be, or will remain, closed the relevant magistrates' court must, in particular, consider whether—

(a) in the case of an order made by virtue of section 161(1)(a), closure is necessary in the interests of public safety because of disorder or likely disorder on the premises, or in the vicinity of and related to, the premises;

(b) in the case of an order made by virtue of section 161(1)(b), closure is necessary to ensure that no public nuisance is, or is likely to be, caused by noise coming from the premises.

(4) In the case of licensed premises, the relevant magistrates' court must notify the relevant licensing authority of any determination it makes under subsection (1)(b).

(5) Subsection (2) does not apply if, before the relevant magistrates' court discharges its functions under that subsection, the premises cease to be relevant premises.

(6) Any order made under subsection (2) ceases to have effect if the premises cease to be relevant premises.

(7) A person commits an offence if, without reasonable excuse, he permits relevant premises to be open in contravention of an order under subsection (2)(b), (c) or (d).

(8) A person guilty of an offence under subsection (7) is liable on summary conviction to imprisonment for a term not exceeding three months or to a fine not exceeding £20,000, or to both.

(9) The powers conferred on a magistrates' court by this section are to be exercised in the place required by the Magistrates' Courts Act 1980 (c. 43) for the hearing of a complaint and may be exercised by a single justice.

(10) Evidence given for the purposes of proceedings under this section must be given on oath.

166 Appeal from decision of magistrates' court

(1) Any person aggrieved by a decision of a magistrates' court under section 165 may appeal to the Crown Court against the decision.

(2) An appeal under subsection (1) must be commenced by notice of appeal given by the appellant to the justices' chief executive for the magistrates' court within the period of 21 days beginning with the day the decision appealed against was made.

167 Review of premises licence following closure order

(1) This section applies where—

(a) a closure order has come into force in relation to premises in respect of which a premises licence has effect, and

(b) the relevant licensing authority has received a notice under section 165(4) (notice of magistrates' court's determination), in relation to the order and any extension of it.

(2) The relevant licensing authority must review the premises licence.

(3) The authority must reach a determination on the review no later than 28 days after the day on which it receives the notice mentioned in subsection (1)(b).

(4) The Secretary of State must by regulations—

(a) require the relevant licensing authority to give, to the holder of the premises licence and each responsible authority, notice of—

(i) the review,

(ii) the closure order and any extension of it, and

(iii) any order made in relation to it under section 165(2);

(b) require the authority to advertise the review and invite representations about it to be made to the authority by responsible authorities and interested parties;

(c) prescribe the period during which representations may be made by the holder of the premises licence, any responsible authority or any interested party;

(d) require any notice under paragraph (a) or advertisement under paragraph (b) to specify that period.

(5) The relevant licensing authority must—

(a) hold a hearing to consider—

(i) the closure order and any extension of it,

(ii) any order under section 165(2), and

(iii) any relevant representations, and

(b) take such of the steps mentioned in subsection (6) (if any) as it considers necessary for the promotion of the licensing objectives.

(6) Those steps are—

(a) to modify the conditions of the premises licence,

(b) to exclude a licensable activity from the scope of the licence,

(c) to remove the designated premises supervisor from the licence,

(d) to suspend the licence for a period not exceeding three months, or

(e) to revoke the licence;

and for this purpose the conditions of a premises licence are modified if any of them is altered or omitted or any new condition is added.

(7) Subsection (5)(b) is subject to sections 19, 20 and 21 (requirement to include certain conditions in premises licences).

(8) Where the authority takes a step within subsection (6)(a) or (b), it may provide that the modification or exclusion is to have effect only for a specified period (not exceeding three months).

(9) In this section "relevant representations" means representations which—

(a) are relevant to one or more of the licensing objectives, and

(b) meet the requirements of subsection (10).

(10) The requirements are—

(a) that the representations are made by the holder of the premises licence, a responsible authority or an interested party within the period prescribed under subsection (4)(c),

(b) that they have not been withdrawn, and

(c) if they are made by an interested party (who is not also a responsible authority), that they are not, in the opinion of the relevant licensing authority, frivolous or vexatious.

(11) Where the relevant licensing authority determines that any representations are frivolous or vexatious, it must notify the person who made them of the reasons for that determination.

(12) Where a licensing authority determines a review under this section it must notify the determination and its reasons for making it to—

(a) the holder of the licence,

(b) any person who made relevant representations, and

(c) the chief officer of police for the police area (or each police area) in which the premises are situated.

(13) Section 168 makes provision about when the determination takes effect.

(14) In this section "interested party" and "responsible authority" have the same meaning as in Part 3.

168 Provision about decisions under section 167

(1) Subject to this section, a decision under section 167 does not have effect until the relevant time.

(2) In this section "the relevant time", in relation to any decision, means—

(a) the end of the period given for appealing against the decision, or

(b) if the decision is appealed against, the time the appeal is disposed of.

(3) Subsections (4) and (5) apply where—

(a) the relevant licensing authority decides on a review under section 167 to take one or more of the steps mentioned in subsection (6)(a) to (d) of that section, and

(b) the premises to which the licence relates have been closed, by virtue of an order under section 165(2)(b), (c) or (d), until that decision was made.

(4) The decision by the relevant licensing authority to take any of the steps mentioned in section 167(6)(a) to (d) takes effect when it is notified to the holder of the licence under section 167(12).

This is subject to subsection (5) and paragraph 18(3) of Schedule 5 (power of magistrates' court to suspend decision pending appeal).

(5) The relevant licensing authority may, on such terms as it thinks fit, suspend the operation of that decision (in whole or in part) until the relevant time.

(6) Subsection (7) applies where—

(a) the relevant licensing authority decides on a review under section 167 to revoke the premises licence, and

(b) the premises to which the licence relates have been closed, by virtue of an order under section 165(2)(b), (c) or (d), until that decision was made.

(7) The premises must remain closed (but the licence otherwise in force) until the relevant time.

This is subject to paragraph 18(4) of Schedule 5 (power of magistrates' court to modify closure order pending appeal).

(8) A person commits an offence if, without reasonable excuse, he allows premises to be open in contravention of subsection (7).

(9) A person guilty of an offence under subsection (8) is liable on summary conviction to imprisonment for a term not exceeding three months or to a fine not exceeding £20,000, or to both.

169 Enforcement of closure order

A constable may use such force as may be necessary for the purposes of closing premises in compliance with a closure order.

170 Exemption of police from liability for damages

(1) A constable is not liable for relevant damages in respect of any act or omission of his in the performance or purported performance of his functions in relation to a closure order or any extension of it.

(2) A chief officer of police is not liable for relevant damages in respect of any act or omission of a constable under his direction or control in the performance or purported performance of a function of the constable's in relation to a closure order or any extension of it.

(3) But neither subsection (1) nor (2) applies—

(a) if the act or omission is shown to have been in bad faith, or

(b) so as to prevent an award of damages in respect of an act or omission on the grounds that the act or omission was unlawful as a result of section 6(1) of the Human Rights Act 1998 (c. 42) (incompatibility of act or omission with Convention rights).

(4) This section does not affect any other exemption from liability for damages (whether at common law or otherwise).

(5) In this section, "relevant damages" means damages awarded in proceedings for judicial review, the tort of negligence or misfeasance in public office.

Interpretation

171 Interpretation of Part 8

(1) This section has effect for the purposes of this Part.

(2) Relevant premises are open if a person who is not within subsection (4) enters the premises and—

(a) he buys or is otherwise supplied with food, drink or anything usually sold on the premises, or

(b) while he is on the premises, they are used for the provision of regulated entertainment.

(3) But in determining whether relevant premises are open the following are to be disregarded—

(a) where no premises licence has effect in respect of the premises, any use of the premises for activities (other than licensable activities) which do not take place during an event period specified in a temporary event notice having effect in respect of the premises,

(b) any use of the premises for a qualifying club activity under and in accordance with a club premises certificate, and

(c) any supply exempted under paragraph 3 of Schedule 2 (certain supplies of hot food and drink by clubs, hotels etc. not a licensable activity) in circumstances where a person will neither be admitted to the premises, nor be supplied as mentioned in sub-paragraph (1)(b) of that paragraph, except by virtue of being a member of a recognised club or a guest of such a member.

(4) A person is within this subsection if he is—

(a) an appropriate person in relation to the premises,

(b) a person who usually lives at the premises, or

(c) a member of the family of a person within paragraph (a) or (b).

(5) The following expressions have the meanings given—

"appropriate person", in relation to any relevant premises, means—

(a) any person who holds a premises licence in respect of the premises,

(b) any designated premises supervisor under such a licence,

(c) the premises user in relation to any temporary event notice which has effect in respect of the premises, or

(d) a manager of the premises;

"closure order" has the meaning given in section 161(2);

"extension", in relation to a closure order, means an extension of the order under section 162;

"manager", in relation to any premises, means a person who works at the premises in a capacity, whether paid or unpaid, which authorises him to close them;

"relevant licensing authority", in relation to any licensed premises, has the same meaning as in Part 3;

"relevant magistrates' court", in relation to any relevant premises, means a magistrates' court acting for the petty sessions area in which the premises are situated;

"relevant premises" has the meaning given in section 161(8);

"responsible senior police officer", in relation to a closure order, means—

(a) the senior police officer who made the order, or

(b) if another senior police officer is designated for the purpose by the chief officer of police for the police area in which the premises are situated, that other officer;

"senior police officer" has the meaning given in section 161(8).

(6) A temporary event notice has effect from the time it is given in accordance with Part 5 until—

(a) the time it is withdrawn,

(b) the time a counter notice is given under that Part, or

(c) the expiry of the event period specified in the temporary event notice,

whichever first occurs.

PART 9

MISCELLANEOUS AND SUPPLEMENTARY

Special occasions

172 Relaxation of opening hours for special occasions

(1) Where the Secretary of State considers that a period ("the celebration period") marks an occasion of exceptional international, national, or local significance, he may make a licensing hours order.

(2) A licensing hours order is an order which provides that during the specified relaxation period premises licences and club premises certificates have effect (to the extent that it is not already the case) as if specified times were included in the opening hours.

(3) An order under this section may—

(a) make provision generally or only in relation to premises in one or more specified areas;

(b) make different provision in respect of different days during the specified relaxation period;

(c) make different provision in respect of different licensable activities.

(4) Before making an order under this section, the Secretary of State must consult such persons as he considers appropriate.

(5) In this section—

"opening hours" means—

(a) in relation to a premises licence, the times during which the premises may be used for licensable activities in accordance with the licence, and

(b) in relation to a club premises certificate, the times during which the premises may be used for qualifying club activities in accordance with the certificate;

"relaxation period" means—

(a) if the celebration period does not exceed four days, that period, or

(b) any part of that period not exceeding four days; and

"specified", in relation to a licensing hours order, means specified in the order.

Exemptions etc.

173 Activities in certain locations not licensable

(1) An activity is not a licensable activity if it is carried on—

(a) aboard an aircraft, hovercraft or railway vehicle engaged on a journey,

(b) aboard a vessel engaged on an international journey,

(c) at an approved wharf at a designated port or hoverport,
(d) at an examination station at a designated airport,
(e) at a royal palace,
(f) at premises which, at the time when the activity is carried on, are permanently or temporarily occupied for the purposes of the armed forces of the Crown,
(g) at premises in respect of which a certificate issued under section 174 (exemption for national security) has effect, or
(h) at such other place as may be prescribed.

(2) For the purposes of subsection (1) the period during which an aircraft, hovercraft, railway vehicle or vessel is engaged on a journey includes—
(a) any period ending with its departure when preparations are being made for the journey, and
(b) any period after its arrival at its destination when it continues to be occupied by those (or any of those) who made the journey (or any part of it).

(3) The Secretary of State may by order designate a port, hoverport or airport for the purposes of subsection (1), if it appears to him to be one at which there is a substantial amount of international passenger traffic.

(4) Any port, airport or hoverport where section 86A or 87 of the Licensing Act 1964 (c. 26) is in operation immediately before the commencement of this section is, on and after that commencement, to be treated for the purposes of subsection (1) as if it were designated.

(5) But provision may by order be made for subsection (4) to cease to have effect in relation to any port, airport or hoverport.

(6) For the purposes of this section—

"approved wharf" has the meaning given by section 20A of the Customs and Excise Management Act 1979 (c. 2);

"designated" means designated by an order under subsection (3);

"examination station" has the meaning given by section 22A of that Act;

"international journey" means—
(a) a journey from a place in the United Kingdom to an immediate destination outside the United Kingdom, or
(b) a journey from a place outside the United Kingdom to an immediate destination in the United Kingdom; and

"railway vehicle" has the meaning given by section 83 of the Railways Act 1993 (c. 43).

174 Certifying of premises on grounds of national security

(1) A Minister of the Crown may issue a certificate under this section in respect of any premises, if he considers that it is appropriate to do so for the purposes of safeguarding national security.

(2) A certificate under this section may identify the premises in question by means of a general description.

(3) A document purporting to be a certificate under this section is to be received in evidence and treated as being a certificate under this section unless the contrary is proved.

(4) A document which purports to be certified by or on behalf of a Minister of the Crown as a true copy of a certificate given by a Minister of the Crown under this section is evidence of that certificate.

(5) A Minister of the Crown may cancel a certificate issued by him, or any other Minister of the Crown, under this section.

(6) The powers conferred by this section on a Minister of the Crown may be exercised only by a Minister who is a member of the Cabinet or by the Attorney General.

(7) In this section "Minister of the Crown" has the meaning given by the Ministers of the Crown Act 1975 (c. 26).

175 Exemption for raffle, tombola, etc.

(1) The conduct of a lottery which, but for this subsection, would to any extent constitute a licensable activity by reason of one or more of the prizes in the lottery consisting of alcohol, is not (for that reason alone) to be treated as constituting a licensable activity if—

- (a) the lottery is promoted as an incident of an exempt entertainment,
- (b) after the deduction of all relevant expenses, the whole proceeds of the entertainment (including those of the lottery) are applied for purposes other than private gain, and
- (c) subsection (2) does not apply.

(2) This subsection applies if—

- (a) the alcohol consists of or includes alcohol not in a sealed container,
- (b) any prize in the lottery is a money prize,
- (c) a ticket or chance in the lottery is sold or issued, or the result of the lottery is declared, other than at the premises where the entertainment takes place and during the entertainment, or
- (d) the opportunity to participate in a lottery or in gaming is the only or main inducement to attend the entertainment.

(3) For the purposes of subsection (1)(b), the following are relevant expenses—

- (a) the expenses of the entertainment, excluding expenses incurred in connection with the lottery,
- (b) the expenses incurred in printing tickets in the lottery,
- (c) such reasonable and proper expenses as the promoters of the lottery appropriate on account of any expenses they incur in buying prizes in the lottery.

(4) In this section—

"exempt entertainment" has the same meaning as in section 3(1) of the Lotteries and Amusements Act 1976 (c. 32);

"gaming" has the meaning given by section 52 of the Gaming Act 1968 (c. 65);

"money" and "ticket" have the meaning given by section 23 of the Lotteries and Amusements Act 1976; and

"private gain", in relation to the proceeds of an entertainment, is to be construed in accordance with section 22 of that Act.

Service areas and garages etc.

176 Prohibition of alcohol sales at service areas, garages etc.

(1) No premises licence, club premises certificate or temporary event notice has effect to authorise the sale by retail or supply of alcohol on or from excluded premises.

(2) In this section "excluded premises" means—

(a) premises situated on land acquired or appropriated by a special road authority, and for the time being used, for the provision of facilities to be used in connection with the use of a special road provided for the use of traffic of class I (with or without other classes); or

(b) premises used primarily as a garage or which form part of premises which are primarily so used.

(3) The Secretary of State may by order amend the definition of excluded premises in subsection (2) so as to include or exclude premises of such description as may be specified in the order.

(4) For the purposes of this section—

(a) "special road" and "special road authority" have the same meaning as in the Highways Act 1980 (c. 66), except that "special road" includes a trunk road to which (by virtue of paragraph 3 of Schedule 23 to that Act) the provisions of that Act apply as if the road were a special road,

(b) "class I" means class I in Schedule 4 to the Highways Act 1980 as varied from time to time by an order under section 17 of that Act, but if that Schedule is amended by such an order so as to add to it a further class of traffic, the order may adapt the reference in subsection (2)(a) to traffic of class I so as to take account of the additional class, and

(c) premises are used as a garage if they are used for one or more of the following—

(i) the retailing of petrol,

(ii) the retailing of derv,

(iii) the sale of motor vehicles,

(iv) the maintenance of motor vehicles.

Small premises

177 Dancing and live music in certain small premises

(1) Subsection (2) applies where—

(a) a premises licence authorises—

(i) the supply of alcohol for consumption on the premises, and

(ii) the provision of music entertainment, and

(b) the premises—

(i) are used primarily for the supply of alcohol for consumption on the premises, and

(ii) have a permitted capacity of not more than 200 persons.

(2) At any time when—

(a) the premises—

(i) are open for the purposes of being used for the supply of alcohol for consumption on the premises, and

(ii) are being used for the provision of music entertainment, and

(b) subsection (4) does not apply,

any licensing authority imposed condition of the premises licence which relates to the provision of music entertainment does not have effect, in relation to the provision of that entertainment, unless it falls within subsection (5) or (6).

(3) Subsection (4) applies where—

(a) a premises licence authorises the provision of music entertainment, and

(b) the premises have a permitted capacity of not more than 200 persons.

(4) At any time between the hours of 8 a.m. and midnight when the premises—

(a) are being used for the provision of music entertainment which consists of—

(i) the performance of unamplified, live music, or

(ii) facilities for enabling persons to take part in entertainment within sub-paragraph (i), but

(b) are not being used for the provision of any other description of regulated entertainment,

any licensing authority imposed condition of the premises licence which relates to the provision of the music entertainment does not have effect, in relation to the provision of that entertainment, unless it falls within subsection (6).

(5) A condition falls within this subsection if the premises licence specifies that the licensing authority which granted the licence considers the imposition of the condition necessary on one or both of the following grounds—

(a) the prevention of crime and disorder,

(b) public safety.

(6) A condition falls within this subsection if, on a review of the premises licence—

(a) it is altered so as to include a statement that this section does not apply to it, or

(b) it is added to the licence and includes such a statement.

(7) This section applies in relation to a club premises certificate as it applies in relation to a premises licence except that, in the application of this section in relation to such a certificate, the definition of "licensing authority imposed condition" in subsection (8) has effect as if for "section 18(3)(b)" to the end there were substituted "section 72(3)(b) (but is not referred to in section 72(2)) or which is imposed by virtue of section 85(3)(b) or 88(3)".

(8) In this section—

"licensing authority imposed condition" means a condition which is imposed by virtue of section 18(3)(b) (but is not referred to in section 18(2)(a)) or which is imposed by virtue of 35(3)(b), 52(3) or 167(5)(b) or in accordance with section 21;

"music entertainment" means—

(a) entertainment of a description falling within, or of a similar description to that falling within, paragraph 2(1)(e) or (g) of Schedule 1, or

(b) facilities enabling persons to take part in entertainment within paragraph (a);

"permitted capacity", in relation to any premises, means—

(a) where a fire certificate issued under the Fire Precautions Act 1971 (c. 40) is in force in respect of the premises and that certificate imposes a requirement under section 6(2)(d) of that Act, the limit on the number of persons who, in accordance with that requirement, may be on the premises at any one time, and

(b) in any other case, the limit on the number of persons who may be on the premises at any one time in accordance with a recommendation made by, or on behalf of, the fire authority for the area in which the premises are situated (or, if the premises are situated in the area of more than one fire authority, those authorities); and

"supply of alcohol" means—

(a) the sale by retail of alcohol, or

(b) the supply of alcohol by or on behalf of a club to, or to the order of, a member of the club.

Rights of freeholders etc.

178 Right of freeholder etc. to be notified of licensing matters

(1) This section applies where—

(a) a person with a property interest in any premises situated in the area of a licensing authority gives notice of his interest to that authority, and

(b) the notice is in the prescribed form and accompanied by the prescribed fee.

(2) The notice has effect for a period of 12 months beginning with the day it is received by the licensing authority.

(3) If a change relating to the premises to which the notice relates is made to the register at a time when the notice has effect, the licensing authority must forthwith notify the person who gave the notice—

(a) of the application, notice or other matter to which the change relates, and

(b) of his right under section 8 to request a copy of the information contained in any entry in the register.

(4) For the purposes of this section a person has a property interest in premises if—

(a) he has a legal interest in the premises as freeholder or leaseholder,

(b) he is a legal mortgagee (within the meaning of the Law of Property Act 1925 (c. 20)) in respect of the premises,

(c) he is in occupation of the premises, or

(d) he has a prescribed interest in the premises.

(5) In this section—

(a) a reference to premises situated in the area of a licensing authority includes a reference to premises partly so situated, and

(b) "register" means the register kept under section 8 by the licensing authority mentioned in subsection (1)(a).

Rights of entry

179 Rights of entry to investigate licensable activities

(1) Where a constable or an authorised person has reason to believe that any premises are being, or are about to be, used for a licensable activity, he may enter the premises with a view to seeing whether the activity is being, or is to be, carried on under and in accordance with an authorisation.

(2) An authorised person exercising the power conferred by this section must, if so requested, produce evidence of his authority to exercise the power.

(3) A person exercising the power conferred by this section may, if necessary, use reasonable force.

(4) A person commits an offence if he intentionally obstructs an authorised person exercising a power conferred by this section.

(5) A person guilty of an offence under subsection (4) is liable on summary conviction to a fine not exceeding level 3 on the standard scale.

(6) In this section—

"authorisation" means—

(a) a premises licence,

(b) a club premises certificate, or

(c) a temporary event notice in respect of which the conditions of section 98(2) to (4) are satisfied; and

"authorised person" means an authorised person within the meaning of Part 3 or 4 or an authorised officer within the meaning of section 108(5).

(7) Nothing in this section applies in relation to premises in respect of which there is a club premises certificate but no other authorisation.

180 Right of entry to investigate offences

(1) A constable may enter and search any premises in respect of which he has reason to believe that an offence under this Act has been, is being or is about to be committed.

(2) A constable exercising a power conferred by this section may, if necessary, use reasonable force.

Appeals

181 Appeals against decisions of licensing authorities

(1) Schedule 5 (which makes provision for appeals against decisions of licensing authorities) has effect.

(2) On an appeal in accordance with that Schedule against a decision of a licensing authority, a magistrates' court may—

(a) dismiss the appeal,
(b) substitute for the decision appealed against any other decision which could have been made by the licensing authority, or
(c) remit the case to the licensing authority to dispose of it in accordance with the direction of the court,

and may make such order as to costs as it thinks fit.

Guidance, hearings etc.

182 Guidance

(1) The Secretary of State must issue guidance ("the licensing guidance") to licensing authorities on the discharge of their functions under this Act.

(2) But the Secretary of State may not issue the licensing guidance unless a draft of it has been laid before, and approved by resolution of, each House of Parliament.

(3) The Secretary of State may, from time to time, revise the licensing guidance.

(4) A revised version of the licensing guidance does not come into force until the Secretary of State lays it before Parliament.

(5) Where either House, before the end of the period of 40 days beginning with the day on which a revised version of the licensing guidance is laid before it, by resolution disapproves that version—
(a) the Secretary of State must, under subsection (3), make such further revisions to the licensing guidance as appear to him to be required in the circumstances, and
(b) before the end of the period of 40 days beginning with the date on which the resolution is made, lay a further revised version of the licensing guidance before Parliament.

(6) In reckoning any period of 40 days for the purposes of subsection (5), no account is to be taken of any time during which—
(a) Parliament is dissolved or prorogued, or
(b) both Houses are adjourned for more than four days.

(7) The Secretary of State must arrange for any guidance issued or revised under this section to be published in such manner as he considers appropriate.

183 Hearings

(1) Regulations may prescribe the procedure to be followed in relation to a hearing held by a licensing authority under this Act and, in particular, may—
(a) require a licensing authority to give notice of hearings to such persons as may be prescribed;
(b) make provision for expedited procedures in urgent cases;
(c) make provision about the rules of evidence which are to apply to hearings;
(d) make provision about the legal representation at hearings of the parties to it;
(e) prescribe the period within which an application, in relation to which a hearing has been held, must be determined or any other step in the procedure must be taken.

(2) But a licensing authority may not make any order as to the costs incurred by a party in connection with a hearing under this Act.

184 Giving of notices, etc.

(1) This section has effect in relation to any document required or authorised by or under this Act to be given to any person ("relevant document").

(2) Where that person is a licensing authority, the relevant document must be given by addressing it to the authority and leaving it at or sending it by post to—

(a) the principal office of the authority, or

(b) any other office of the authority specified by it as one at which it will accept documents of the same description as that document.

(3) In any other case the relevant document may be given to the person in question by delivering it to him, or by leaving it at his proper address, or by sending it by post to him at that address.

(4) A relevant document may—

(a) in the case of a body corporate (other than a licensing authority), be given to the secretary or clerk of that body;

(b) in the case of a partnership, be given to a partner or a person having the control or management of the partnership business;

(c) in the case of an unincorporated association (other than a partnership), be given to an officer of the association.

(5) For the purposes of this section and section 7 of the Interpretation Act 1978 (c. 30) (service of documents by post) in its application to this section, the proper address of any person to whom a relevant document is to be given is his last known address, except that—

(a) in the case of a body corporate or its secretary or clerk, it is the address of the registered office of that body or its principal office in the United Kingdom,

(b) in the case of a partnership, a partner or a person having control or management of the partnership business, it is that of the principal office of the partnership in the United Kingdom, and

(c) in the case of an unincorporated association (other than a partnership) or any officer of the association, it is that of its principal office in the United Kingdom.

(6) But if a relevant document is given to a person in his capacity as the holder of a premises licence, club premises certificate or personal licence, or as the designated premises supervisor under a premises licence, his relevant registered address is also to be treated, for the purposes of this section and section 7 of the Interpretation Act 1978 (c. 30), as his proper address.

(7) In subsection (6) "relevant registered address", in relation to such a person, means the address given for that person in the record for the licence or certificate (as the case may be) which is contained in the register kept under section 8 by the licensing authority which granted the licence or certificate.

(8) The following provisions of the Local Government Act 1972 (c. 70)do not apply in relation to the service of a relevant document—

(a) section 231 (service of notices on local authorities etc.),

(b) section 233 (service of notices by local authorities).

185 Provision of information

(1) This section applies to information which is held by or on behalf of a licensing authority or a responsible authority (including information obtained by or on behalf of the authority before the coming into force of this section).

(2) Information to which this section applies may be supplied—

(a) to a licensing authority, or

(b) to a responsible authority,

for the purposes of facilitating the exercise of the authority's functions under this Act.

(3) Information obtained by virtue of this section must not be further disclosed except to a licensing authority or responsible authority for the purposes mentioned in subsection (2).

(4) In this section "responsible authority" means a responsible authority within the meaning of Part 3 or 4.

General provisions about offences

186 Proceedings for offences

(1) In this section "offence" means an offence under this Act.

(2) Proceedings for an offence may be instituted—

(a) by a licensing authority,

(b) by the Director of Public Prosecutions, or

(c) in the case of an offence under section 146 or 147 (sale of alcohol to children), by a local weights and measures authority (within the meaning of section 69 of the Weights and Measures Act 1985 (c. 72)).

(3) In relation to any offence, section 127(1) of the Magistrates' Courts Act 1980 (information to be laid within six months of offence) is to have effect as if for the reference to six months there were substituted a reference to 12 months.

187 Offences by bodies corporate etc.

(1) If an offence committed by a body corporate is shown—

(a) to have been committed with the consent or connivance of an officer, or

(b) to be attributable to any neglect on his part,

the officer as well as the body corporate is guilty of the offence and liable to be proceeded against and punished accordingly.

(2) If the affairs of a body corporate are managed by its members, subsection (1) applies in relation to the acts and defaults of a member in connection with his functions of management as if he were a director of the body.

(3) In subsection (1) "officer", in relation to a body corporate, means—

(a) a director, member of the committee of management, chief executive, manager, secretary or other similar officer of the body, or a person purporting to act in any such capacity, or

(b) an individual who is a controller of the body.

(4) If an offence committed by a partnership is shown—

(a) to have been committed with the consent or connivance of a partner, or

(b) to be attributable to any neglect on his part,

the partner as well as the partnership is guilty of the offence and liable to be proceeded against and punished accordingly.

(5) In subsection (4) "partner" includes a person purporting to act as a partner.

(6) If an offence committed by an unincorporated association (other than a partnership) is shown—

(a) to have been committed with the consent or connivance of an officer of the association or a member of its governing body, or

(b) to be attributable to any neglect on the part of such an officer or member,

that officer or member as well as the association is guilty of the offence and liable to be proceeded against and punished accordingly.

(7) Regulations may provide for the application of any provision of this section, with such modifications as the Secretary of State considers appropriate, to a body corporate or unincorporated association formed or recognised under the law of a territory outside the United Kingdom.

(8) In this section "offence" means an offence under this Act.

188 Jurisdiction and procedure in respect of offences

(1) A fine imposed on an unincorporated association on its conviction for an offence is to be paid out of the funds of the association.

(2) Proceedings for an offence alleged to have been committed by an unincorporated association must be brought in the name of the association (and not in that of any of its members).

(3) Rules of court relating to the service of documents are to have effect as if the association were a body corporate.

(4) In proceedings for an offence brought against an unincorporated association, section 33 of the Criminal Justice Act 1925 (c. 86) and Schedule 3 to the Magistrates' Courts Act 1980 (c. 43) (procedure) apply as they do in relation to a body corporate.

(5) Proceedings for an offence may be taken—

(a) against a body corporate or unincorporated association at any place at which it has a place of business;

(b) against an individual at any place where he is for the time being.

(6) Subsection (5) does not affect any jurisdiction exercisable apart from this section.

(7) In this section "offence" means an offence under this Act.

Vessels, vehicles and moveable structures

189 Vessels, vehicles and moveable structures

(1) This Act applies in relation to a vessel which is not permanently moored or berthed as if it were premises situated in the place where it is usually moored or berthed.

(2) Where a vehicle which is not permanently situated in the same place is, or is proposed to be, used for one or more licensable activities while parked at a particular place, the vehicle is to be treated for the purposes of this Act as if it were premises situated at that place.

(3) Where a moveable structure which is not permanently situated in the same place is, or is proposed to be, used for one or more licensable activities while set in a particular place, the structure is to be treated for the purposes of this Act as if it were premises situated at that place.

(4) Where subsection (2) applies in relation to the same vehicle, or subsection (3) applies in relation to the same structure, in respect of more than one place, the premises which by virtue of that subsection are situated at each such place are to be treated as separate premises.

(5) Sections 29 to 31 (which make provision in respect of provisional statements relating to premises licences) do not apply in relation to a vessel, vehicle or structure to which this section applies.

Interpretation

190 Location of sales

(1) This section applies where the place where a contract for the sale of alcohol is made is different from the place where the alcohol is appropriated to the contract.

(2) For the purposes of this Act the sale of alcohol is to be treated as taking place where the alcohol is appropriated to the contract.

191 Meaning of "alcohol"

(1) In this Act, "alcohol" means spirits, wine, beer, cider or any other fermented, distilled or spirituous liquor, but does not include—

- (a) alcohol which is of a strength not exceeding 0.5% at the time of the sale or supply in question,
- (b) perfume,
- (c) flavouring essences recognised by the Commissioners of Customs and Excise as not being intended for consumption as or with dutiable alcoholic liquor,
- (d) the aromatic flavouring essence commonly known as Angostura bitters,
- (e) alcohol which is, or is included in, a medicinal product,
- (f) denatured alcohol,
- (g) methyl alcohol,
- (h) naphtha, or
- (i) alcohol contained in liqueur confectionery.

(2) In this section—

"denatured alcohol" has the same meaning as in section 5 of the Finance Act 1995 (c. 4);

"dutiable alcoholic liquor" has the same meaning as in the Alcoholic Liquor Duties Act 1979 (c. 4);

"liqueur confectionery" means confectionery which—

(a) contains alcohol in a proportion not greater than 0.2 litres of alcohol (of a strength not exceeding 57%) per kilogram of the confectionery, and

(b) either consists of separate pieces weighing not more than 42g or is designed to be broken into such pieces for the purpose of consumption;

"medicinal product" has the same meaning as in section 130 of the Medicines Act 1968 (c. 67); and

"strength" is to be construed in accordance with section 2 of the Alcoholic Liquor Duties Act 1979.

192 Meaning of "sale by retail"

(1) For the purposes of this Act "sale by retail", in relation to any alcohol, means a sale of alcohol to any person, other than a sale of alcohol that—

(a) is within subsection (2),

(b) is made from premises owned by the person making the sale, or occupied by him under a lease to which the provisions of Part 2 of the Landlord and Tenant Act 1954 (c. 56) (security of tenure) apply, and

(c) is made for consumption off the premises.

(2) A sale of alcohol is within this subsection if it is—

(a) to a trader for the purposes of his trade,

(b) to a club, which holds a club premises certificate, for the purposes of that club,

(c) to the holder of a personal licence for the purpose of making sales authorised by a premises licence,

(d) to the holder of a premises licence for the purpose of making sales authorised by that licence, or

(e) to the premises user in relation to a temporary event notice for the purpose of making sales authorised by that notice.

193 Other definitions

In this Act—

"beer" has the same meaning as in the Alcoholic Liquor Duties Act 1979 (c. 4);

"cider" has the same meaning as in that Act;

"crime prevention objective" means the licensing objective mentioned in section 4(2)(a) (prevention of crime and disorder);

"licensed premises" means premises in respect of which a premises licence has effect;

"licensing functions" is to be construed in accordance with section 4(1);

"order", except so far as the contrary intention appears, means an order made by the Secretary of State;

"premises" means any place and includes a vehicle, vessel or moveable structure;

"prescribed" means prescribed by regulations;

"recognised club" means a club which satisfies conditions 1 to 3 of the general conditions in section 62;

"regulations" means regulations made by the Secretary of State;

"vehicle" means a vehicle intended or adapted for use on roads;

"vessel" includes a ship, boat, raft or other apparatus constructed or adapted for floating on water;

"wine" means—

(a) "wine" within the meaning of the Alcoholic Liquor Duties Act 1979, and

(b) "made-wine" within the meaning of that Act;

"working day" means any day other than a Saturday, a Sunday, Christmas Day, Good Friday or a day which is a bank holiday under the Banking and Financial Dealings Act 1971 (c. 80) in England and Wales.

194 Index of defined expressions

In this Act the following expressions are defined or otherwise explained by the provisions indicated—

Expression	*Interpretation provision*
alcohol	section 191
associate member	section 67(2)
authorised person, in Part 3	section 13
authorised person, in Part 4	section 69
beer	section 193
cider	section 193
club premises certificate	section 60
conviction, in Part 6	section 114
crime prevention objective	section 193
designated premises supervisor	section 15
foreign offence, in Part 6	section 113
given, in relation to a notice, etc.	section 184
guest	section 67(1)
interested party, in Part 3	section 13
interested party, in Part 4	section 69
interim authority notice	section 47
late night refreshment	Schedule 2
licensable activity	section 1(1)
licensed premises	section 193

Expression	*Interpretation provision*
licensing authority	section 3(1)
licensing authority's area	section 3(2)
licensing functions	sections 4(1) and 193
licensing objectives	section 4(2)
order	section 193
permitted temporary activity	section 98
personal licence	section 111(1)
premises	section 193
premises licence	section 11
premises user, in relation to a temporary event notice	section 100(2)
prescribed	section 193
provisional statement	section 29(3)
qualifying club	section 61
qualifying club activity	section 1(2)
recognised club	section 193
regulated entertainment	Schedule 1
regulations	section 193
relevant licensing authority, in Part 3	section 12
relevant licensing authority, in Part 4	section 68
relevant licensing authority, in Part 5	section 99
relevant licensing authority, in Part 6	section 112
relevant offence, in Part 6	section 113
responsible authority, in Part 3	section 13
responsible authority, in Part 4	section 69
sale by retail, in relation to alcohol	section 192
secretary, in Part 4	section 70
supply of alcohol, in Part 3	section 14
supply of alcohol to members or guests, in relation to a club, in Part 4	section 70
temporary event notice	section 100(1)
vehicle	section 193
vessel	section 193
wine	section 193
working day	section 193

Supplementary and general

195 Crown application

(1) This Act binds the Crown and has effect in relation to land in which there is—

- (a) an interest belonging to Her Majesty in right of the Crown,
- (b) an interest belonging to a government department, or
- (c) an interest held in trust for Her Majesty for the purposes of such a department.

(2) This Act also applies to—

- (a) land which is vested in, but not occupied by, Her Majesty in right of the Duchy of Lancaster, and
- (b) land which is vested in, but not occupied by, the possessor for the time being of the Duchy of Cornwall.

(3) No contravention by the Crown of any provision made by or under this Act makes the Crown criminally liable; but the High Court may declare unlawful any act or omission of the Crown which constitutes such a contravention.

(4) Provision made by or under this Act applies to persons in the public service of the Crown as it applies to other persons.

(5) But nothing in this Act affects Her Majesty in Her private capacity.

196 Removal of privileges and exemptions

No privilege or exemption mentioned in section 199(a) or (b) of the Licensing Act 1964 (c. 26) (University of Cambridge and the Vintners of the City of London) operates to exempt any person from the requirements of this Act.

197 Regulations and orders

(1) Any power of the Secretary of State to make regulations or an order under this Act is exercisable by statutory instrument.

(2) Regulations or an order under this Act—

- (a) may include incidental, supplementary, consequential or transitional provision or savings;
- (b) may make provision generally or only in relation to specified cases;
- (c) may make different provision for different purposes.

(3) A statutory instrument containing regulations or an order under this Act, other than one containing—

- (a) an order under section 5(2) (order appointing start of first period for which statement of licensing policy to be prepared),
- (b) an order under section 100(8)(alteration of maximum temporary event period),
- (c) an order under section 107(12) (alteration of limit on number of temporary event notices),
- (d) an order under section 172 (relaxation of opening hours for special occasions),
- (e) an order under section 176(3) (order amending definition of "excluded premises" where alcohol sales are prohibited),

(f) an order under section 201 (commencement), or

(g) an order under paragraph 4 of Schedule 1 (power to amend meaning of regulated entertainment),

is subject to annulment in pursuance of a resolution of either House of Parliament.

(4) A statutory instrument containing an order within subsection (3)(b), (c), (d), (e) or (g) is not to be made unless a draft of the instrument containing the order has been laid before and approved by a resolution of each House of Parliament.

(5) If a draft of an order within subsection (3)(d) would, apart from this subsection, be treated for the purposes of the Standing Orders of either House of Parliament as a hybrid instrument, it is to proceed in that House as if it were not such an instrument.

198 Minor and consequential amendments

(1) Schedule 6 (which makes minor and consequential amendments) has effect.

(2) The Secretary of State may, in consequence of any provision of this Act or of any instrument made under it, by order make such amendments (including repeals or revocations) as appear to him to be appropriate in—

(a) any Act passed, or

(b) any subordinate legislation (within the meaning of the Interpretation Act 1978 (c. 30) made,

before that provision comes into force.

199 Repeals

The enactments mentioned in Schedule 7 (which include provisions that are spent) are repealed to the extent specified.

200 Transitional provision etc.

Schedule 8 (which makes transitional and transitory provision and savings) has effect.

201 Short title, commencement and extent

(1) This Act may be cited as the Licensing Act 2003.

(2) The preceding provisions (and the Schedules) come into force in accordance with provision made by order.

(3) Subject to subsections (4) and (5), this Act extends to England and Wales only.

(4) Section 155(1) also extends to Northern Ireland.

(5) An amendment or repeal contained in Schedule 6 or 7 has the same extent as the enactment to which it relates.

SCHEDULES

SCHEDULE 1

Section 1

PROVISION OF REGULATED ENTERTAINMENT

PART 1

GENERAL DEFINITIONS

The provision of regulated entertainment

1 (1) For the purposes of this Act the "provision of regulated entertainment" means the provision of—

(a) entertainment of a description falling within paragraph 2, or

(b) entertainment facilities falling within paragraph 3,

where the conditions in sub-paragraphs (2) and (3) are satisfied.

(2) The first condition is that the entertainment is, or entertainment facilities are, provided—

(a) to any extent for members of the public or a section of the public,

(b) exclusively for members of a club which is a qualifying club in relation to the provision of regulated entertainment, or for members of such a club and their guests, or

(c) in any case not falling within paragraph (a) or (b), for consideration and with a view to profit.

(3) The second condition is that the premises on which the entertainment is, or entertainment facilities are, provided are made available for the purpose, or for purposes which include the purpose, of enabling the entertainment concerned (whether of a description falling within paragraph 2(1) or paragraph 3(2)) to take place.

To the extent that the provision of entertainment facilities consists of making premises available, the premises are to be regarded for the purposes of this sub-paragraph as premises "on which" entertainment facilities are provided.

(4) For the purposes of sub-paragraph (2)(c), entertainment is, or entertainment facilities are, to be regarded as provided for consideration only if any charge—

(a) is made by or on behalf of—

(i) any person concerned in the organisation or management of that entertainment, or

(ii) any person concerned in the organisation or management of those facilities who is also concerned in the organisation or management of the entertainment within paragraph 3(2) in which those facilities enable persons to take part, and

(b) is paid by or on behalf of some or all of the persons for whom that entertainment is, or those facilities are, provided.

(5) In sub-paragraph (4), "charge" includes any charge for the provision of goods or services.

(6) For the purposes of sub-paragraph (4)(a), where the entertainment consists of the performance of live music or the playing of recorded music, a person performing or playing the music is not concerned in the organisation or management of the entertainment by reason only that he does one or more of the following—

(a) chooses the music to be performed or played,

(b) determines the manner in which he performs or plays it,

(c) provides any facilities for the purposes of his performance or playing of the music.

(7) This paragraph is subject to Part 2 of this Schedule (exemptions).

Entertainment

2 (1) The descriptions of entertainment are—

(a) a performance of a play,

(b) an exhibition of a film,

(c) an indoor sporting event,

(d) a boxing or wrestling entertainment,

(e) a performance of live music,

(f) any playing of recorded music,

(g) a performance of dance,

(h) entertainment of a similar description to that falling within paragraph (e), (f) or (g),

where the entertainment takes place in the presence of an audience and is provided for the purpose, or for purposes which include the purpose, of entertaining that audience.

(2) Any reference in sub-paragraph (1) to an audience includes a reference to spectators.

(3) This paragraph is subject to Part 3 of this Schedule (interpretation).

Entertainment facilities

3 (1) In this Schedule, "entertainment facilities" means facilities for enabling persons to take part in entertainment of a description falling within sub-paragraph (2) for the purpose, or for purposes which include the purpose, of being entertained.

(2) The descriptions of entertainment are—

(a) making music,

(b) dancing,

(c) entertainment of a similar description to that falling within paragraph (a) or (b).

(3) This paragraph is subject to Part 3 of this Schedule (interpretation).

Power to amend Schedule

4 The Secretary of State may by order amend this Schedule for the purpose of modifying—

(a) the descriptions of entertainment specified in paragraph 2, or

(b) the descriptions of entertainment specified in paragraph 3,

and for this purpose "modify" includes adding, varying or removing any description.

Part 2

Exemptions

Film exhibitions for the purposes of advertisement, information, education, etc.

5 The provision of entertainment consisting of the exhibition of a film is not to be regarded as the provision of regulated entertainment for the purposes of this Act if its sole or main purpose is to—

(a) demonstrate any product,

(b) advertise any goods or services, or

(c) provide information, education or instruction.

Film exhibitions: museums and art galleries

6 The provision of entertainment consisting of the exhibition of a film is not to be regarded as the provision of regulated entertainment for the purposes of this Act if it consists of or forms part of an exhibit put on show for any purposes of a museum or art gallery.

Music incidental to certain other activities

7 The provision of entertainment consisting of the performance of live music or the playing of recorded music is not to be regarded as the provision of regulated entertainment for the purposes of this Act to the extent that it is incidental to some other activity which is not itself—

(a) a description of entertainment falling within paragraph 2, or

(b) the provision of entertainment facilities.

Use of television or radio receivers

8 The provision of any entertainment or entertainment facilities is not to be regarded as the provision of regulated entertainment for the purposes of this Act to the extent that it consists of the simultaneous reception and playing of a programme included in a programme service within the meaning of the Broadcasting Act 1990 (c. 42).

Religious services, places of worship etc.

9 The provision of any entertainment or entertainment facilities—

(a) for the purposes of, or for purposes incidental to, a religious meeting or service, or

(b) at a place of public religious worship,

is not to be regarded as the provision of regulated entertainment for the purposes of this Act.

Garden fêtes, etc.

10 (1) The provision of any entertainment or entertainment facilities at a garden fête, or at a function or event of a similar character, is not to be regarded as the provision of regulated entertainment for the purposes of this Act.

(2) But sub-paragraph (1) does not apply if the fête, function or event is promoted with a view to applying the whole or part of its proceeds for purposes of private gain.

(3) In sub-paragraph (2) "private gain", in relation to the proceeds of a fête, function or event, is to be construed in accordance with section 22 of the Lotteries and Amusements Act 1976 (c. 32).

Morris dancing etc.

11 The provision of any entertainment or entertainment facilities is not to be regarded as the provision of regulated entertainment for the purposes of this Act to the extent that it consists of the provision of—

(a) a performance of morris dancing or any dancing of a similar nature or a performance of unamplified, live music as an integral part of such a performance , or

(b) facilities for enabling persons to take part in entertainment of a description falling within paragraph (a).

Vehicles in motion

12 The provision of any entertainment or entertainment facilities—

(a) on premises consisting of or forming part of a vehicle, and

(b) at a time when the vehicle is not permanently or temporarily parked,

is not to be regarded as the provision of regulated entertainment for the purposes of this Act.

Part 3

Interpretation

General

13 This Part has effect for the purposes of this Schedule.

Plays

14 (1) A "performance of a play" means a performance of any dramatic piece, whether involving improvisation or not,—

(a) which is given wholly or in part by one or more persons actually present and performing, and

(b) in which the whole or a major proportion of what is done by the person or persons performing, whether by way of speech, singing or action, involves the playing of a role.

(2) In this paragraph, "performance" includes rehearsal (and "performing" is to be construed accordingly).

Film exhibitions

15 An "exhibition of a film" means any exhibition of moving pictures.

Indoor sporting events

16 (1) An "indoor sporting event" is a sporting event—

(a) which takes place wholly inside a building, and

(b) at which the spectators present at the event are accommodated wholly inside that building.

(2) In this paragraph—

"building" means any roofed structure (other than a structure with a roof which may be opened or closed) and includes a vehicle, vessel or moveable structure,

"sporting event" means any contest, exhibition or display of any sport, and

"sport" includes—

(a) any game in which physical skill is the predominant factor, and

(b) any form of physical recreation which is also engaged in for purposes of competition or display.

Boxing or wrestling entertainments

17 A "boxing or wrestling entertainment" is any contest, exhibition or display of boxing or wrestling.

Music

18 "Music" includes vocal or instrumental music or any combination of the two.

SCHEDULE 2

Section 1

PROVISION OF LATE NIGHT REFRESHMENT

The provision of late night refreshment

1 (1) For the purposes of this Act, a person "provides late night refreshment" if—

(a) at any time between the hours of 11.00 p.m. and 5.00 a.m., he supplies hot food or hot drink to members of the public, or a section of the public, on or from any premises, whether for consumption on or off the premises, or

(b) at any time between those hours when members of the public, or a section of the public, are admitted to any premises, he supplies, or holds himself out as willing to supply, hot food or hot drink to any persons, or to persons of a particular description, on or from those premises, whether for consumption on or off the premises,

unless the supply is an exempt supply by virtue of paragraph 3, 4 or 5.

(2) References in this Act to the "provision of late night refreshment" are to be construed in accordance with sub-paragraph (1).

(3) This paragraph is subject to the following provisions of this Schedule.

Hot food or hot drink

2 Food or drink supplied on or from any premises is "hot" for the purposes of this Schedule if the food or drink, or any part of it,—

(a) before it is supplied, is heated on the premises or elsewhere for the purpose of enabling it to be consumed at a temperature above the ambient air temperature and, at the time of supply, is above that temperature, or

(b) after it is supplied, may be heated on the premises for the purpose of enabling it to be consumed at a temperature above the ambient air temperature.

Exempt supplies: clubs, hotels etc. and employees

3 (1) The supply of hot food or hot drink on or from any premises at any time is an exempt supply for the purposes of paragraph 1(1) if, at that time, a person will neither—

(a) be admitted to the premises, nor

(b) be supplied with hot food or hot drink on or from the premises,

except by virtue of being a person of a description falling within sub-paragraph (2).

(2) The descriptions are that—

(a) he is a member of a recognised club,

(b) he is a person staying at a particular hotel, or at particular comparable premises, for the night in question,

(c) he is an employee of a particular employer,

(d) he is engaged in a particular trade, he is a member of a particular profession or he follows a particular vocation,

(e) he is a guest of a person falling within any of paragraphs (a) to (d).

(3) The premises which, for the purposes of sub-paragraph (2)(b), are comparable to a hotel are—

(a) a guest house, lodging house or hostel,

(b) a caravan site or camping site, or

(c) any other premises the main purpose of maintaining which is the provision of facilities for overnight accommodation.

Exempt supplies: premises licensed under certain other Acts

4 The supply of hot food or hot drink on or from any premises is an exempt supply for the purposes of paragraph 1(1) if it takes place during a period for which—

(a) the premises may be used for a public exhibition of a kind described in section 21(1) of the Greater London Council (General Powers) Act 1966 (c. xxviii) by virtue of a licence under that section, or

(b) the premises may be used as near beer premises within the meaning of section 14 of the London Local Authorities Act 1995 (c. x) by virtue of a licence under section 16 of that Act.

Miscellaneous exempt supplies

5 (1) The following supplies of hot food or hot drink are exempt supplies for the purposes of paragraph 1(1)—

(a) the supply of hot drink which consists of or contains alcohol,

(b) the supply of hot drink by means of a vending machine,

(c) the supply of hot food or hot drink free of charge,

(d) the supply of hot food or hot drink by a registered charity or a person authorised by a registered charity,

(e) the supply of hot food or hot drink on a vehicle at a time when the vehicle is not permanently or temporarily parked.

(2) Hot drink is supplied by means of a vending machine for the purposes of sub-paragraph (1)(b) only if—

(a) the payment for the hot drink is inserted into the machine by a member of the public, and

(b) the hot drink is supplied directly by the machine to a member of the public.

(3) Hot food or hot drink is not to be regarded as supplied free of charge for the purposes of sub-paragraph (1)(c) if, in order to obtain the hot food or hot drink, a charge must be paid—

(a) for admission to any premises, or

(b) for some other item.

(4) In sub-paragraph (1)(d) "registered charity" means—

(a) a charity which is registered under section 3 of the Charities Act 1993 (c. 10), or

(b) a charity which by virtue of subsection (5) of that section is not required to be so registered.

Clubs which are not recognised clubs: members and guests

6 For the purposes of this Schedule—

(a) the supply of hot food or hot drink to a person as being a member, or the guest of a member, of a club which is not a recognised club is to be taken to be a supply to a member of the public, and

(b) the admission of any person to any premises as being such a member or guest is to be taken to be the admission of a member of the public.

SCHEDULE 3

Section 8

MATTERS TO BE ENTERED IN LICENSING REGISTER

The licensing register kept by a licensing authority under section 8 must contain a record of the following matters—

(a) any application made to the licensing authority under section 17 (grant of premises licence),
(b) any application made to it under section 25 (theft etc. of premises licence or summary),
(c) any notice given to it under section 28 (surrender of premises licence),
(d) any application made to it under section 29 (provisional notice in respect of premises),
(e) any notice given to it under section 33 (change of name, etc. of holder of premises licence),
(f) any application made to it under section 34 (variation of premises licence),
(g) any application made to it under section 37 (variation of licence to specify individual as premises supervisor),
(h) any notice given to it under section 41 (request from designated premises supervisor for removal from premises licence),
(i) any application made to it under section 42 (transfer of premises licence),
(j) any notice given to it under section 47 (interim authority notice),
(k) any application made to it under section 51 (review of premises licence),
(l) any application made to it under section 71 (application for club premises certificate),
(m) any application made to it under section 79 (theft, loss, etc. of certificate or summary),
(n) any notice given to it under section 81 (surrender of club premises certificate),
(o) any notice given to it under section 82 or 83 (notification of change of name etc.),
(p) any application made to it under section 84 (application to vary club premises certificate),
(q) any application made to it under section 87 (application for review of club premises certificate),
(r) any notice given to it under section 103 (withdrawal of temporary event notice),
(s) any counter notice given by it under section 105 (counter notice following police objection to temporary event notice),
(t) any copy of a temporary event notice give to it under section 106 (notice given following the making of modifications to a temporary event notice with police consent),
(u) any application made to it under section 110 (theft etc. of temporary event notice),
(v) any notice given to it under section 116 (surrender of personal licence),
(w) any application made to it under section 117 (grant or renewal of personal licence),
(x) any application made to it under section 126 (theft, loss or destruction of personal licence),
(y) any notice given to it under section 127 (change of name, etc. of personal licence holder),
(z) any notice given to it under section 165(4) (magistrates' court to notify any determination made after closure order),
(zi) any application under paragraph 2 of Schedule 8 (application for conversion of old licences into premises licence),
(zii) any application under paragraph 14 of that Schedule (application for conversion of club certificate into club premises certificate).

SCHEDULE 4

Section 113

PERSONAL LICENCE: RELEVANT OFFENCES

1 An offence under this Act.

2 An offence under any of the following enactments—

(a) Schedule 12 to the London Government Act 1963 (c. 33) (public entertainment licensing);

(b) the Licensing Act 1964 (c. 26);
(c) the Private Places of Entertainment (Licensing) Act 1967 (c. 19);
(d) section 13 of the Theatres Act 1968 (c. 54);
(e) the Late Night Refreshment Houses Act 1969 (c. 53);
(f) section 6 of, or Schedule 1 to, the Local Government (Miscellaneous Provisions) Act 1982 (c. 30);
(g) the Licensing (Occasional Permissions) Act 1983 (c. 24);
(h) the Cinemas Act 1985 (c. 13);
(i) the London Local Authorities Act 1990 (c. vii).

3 An offence under the Firearms Act 1968 (c. 27).

4 An offence under section 1 of the Trade Descriptions Act 1968 (c. 29) (false trade description of goods) in circumstances where the goods in question are or include alcohol.

5 An offence under any of the following provisions of the Theft Act 1968 (c. 60)—
(a) section 1 (theft);
(b) section 8 (robbery);
(c) section 9 (burglary);
(d) section 10 (aggravated burglary);
(e) section 11 (removal of articles from places open to the public);
(f) section 12A (aggravated vehicle-taking), in circumstances where subsection (2)(b) of that section applies and the accident caused the death of any person;
(g) section 13 (abstracting of electricity);
(h) section 15 (obtaining property by deception);
(i) section 15A (obtaining a money transfer by deception);
(j) section 16 (obtaining pecuniary advantage by deception);
(k) section 17 (false accounting);
(l) section 19 (false statements by company directors etc.);
(m) section 20 (suppression, etc. of documents);
(n) section 21 (blackmail);
(o) section 22 (handling stolen goods);
(p) section 24A (dishonestly retaining a wrongful credit);
(q) section 25 (going equipped for stealing etc.).

6 An offence under section 7(2) of the Gaming Act 1968 (c. 65) (allowing child to take part in gaming on premises licensed for the sale of alcohol).

7 An offence under any of the following provisions of the Misuse of Drugs Act 1971 (c. 38)—
(a) section 4(2) (production of a controlled drug);
(b) section 4(3) (supply of a controlled drug);
(c) section 5(3) (possession of a controlled drug with intent to supply);
(d) section 8 (permitting activities to take place on premises).

8 An offence under either of the following provisions of the Theft Act 1978 (c. 31)—
(a) section 1 (obtaining services by deception);
(b) section 2 (evasion of liability by deception).

9 An offence under either of the following provisions of the Customs and Excise Management Act 1979 (c. 2)—

(a) section 170 (disregarding subsection (1)(a)) (fraudulent evasion of duty etc.);

(b) section 170B (taking preparatory steps for evasion of duty).

10 An offence under either of the following provisions of the Tobacco Products Duty Act 1979 (c. 7)—

(a) section 8G (possession and sale of unmarked tobacco);

(b) section 8H (use of premises for sale of unmarked tobacco).

11 An offence under the Forgery and Counterfeiting Act 1981 (c. 45) (other than an offence under section 18 or 19 of that Act).

12 An offence under the Firearms (Amendment) Act 1988 (c. 45).

13 An offence under any of the following provisions of the Copyright, Designs and Patents Act 1988 (c. 48)—

(a) section 107(1)(d)(iii) (public exhibition in the course of a business of article infringing copyright);

(b) section 107(3) (infringement of copyright by public performance of work etc.);

(c) section 198(2) (broadcast etc. of recording of performance made without sufficient consent);

(d) section 297(1) (fraudulent reception of transmission);

(e) section 297A(1) (supply etc. of unauthorised decoder).

14 An offence under any of the following provisions of the Road Traffic Act 1988 (c. 52)—

(a) section 3A (causing death by careless driving while under the influence of drink or drugs);

(b) section 4 (driving etc. a vehicle when under the influence of drink or drugs);

(c) section 5 (driving etc. a vehicle with alcohol concentration above prescribed limit).

15 An offence under either of the following provisions of the Food Safety Act 1990 (c. 16) in circumstances where the food in question is or includes alcohol—

(a) section 14 (selling food or drink not of the nature, substance or quality demanded);

(b) section 15 (falsely describing or presenting food or drink).

16 An offence under section 92(1) or (2) of the Trade Marks Act 1994 (c. 26) (unauthorised use of trade mark, etc. in relation to goods) in circumstances where the goods in question are or include alcohol.

17 An offence under the Firearms (Amendment) Act 1997 (c. 5).

18 A sexual offence, within the meaning of section 161(2) of the Powers of Criminal Courts (Sentencing) Act 2000 (c. 6).

19 A violent offence, within the meaning of section 161(3) of that Act.

20 An offence under section 3 of the Private Security Industry Act 2001 (c. 12) (engaging in certain activities relating to security without a licence).

SCHEDULE 5

Section 181

APPEALS

PART 1

PREMISES LICENCES

Rejection of applications relating to premises licences

1 Where a licensing authority—

(a) rejects an application for a premises licence under section 18,

(b) rejects (in whole or in part) an application to vary a premises licence under section 35,

(c) rejects an application to vary a premises licence to specify an individual as the premises supervisor under section 39, or

(d) rejects an application to transfer a premises licence under section 44,

the applicant may appeal against the decision.

Decision to grant premises licence or impose conditions etc.

2 (1) This paragraph applies where a licensing authority grants a premises licence under section 18.

(2) The holder of the licence may appeal against any decision—

(a) to impose conditions on the licence under subsection (2)(a) or (3)(b) of that section, or

(b) to take any step mentioned in subsection (4)(b) or (c) of that section (exclusion of licensable activity or refusal to specify person as premises supervisor).

(3) Where a person who made relevant representations in relation to the application desires to contend—

(a) that the licence ought not to have been granted, or

(b) that, on granting the licence, the licensing authority ought to have imposed different or additional conditions, or to have taken a step mentioned in subsection (4)(b) or (c) of that section,

he may appeal against the decision.

(4) In sub-paragraph (3) "relevant representations" has the meaning given in section 18(6).

Issue of provisional statement

3 (1) This paragraph applies where a provisional statement is issued under subsection (3)(c) of section 31.

(2) An appeal against the decision may be made by—

(a) the applicant, or

(b) any person who made relevant representations in relation to the application.

(3) In sub-paragraph (2) "relevant representations" has the meaning given in subsection (5) of that section.

Variation of licence under section 35

4 (1) This paragraph applies where an application to vary a premises licence is granted (in whole or in part) under section 35.

(2) The applicant may appeal against any decision to modify the conditions of the licence under subsection (4)(a) of that section.

(3) Where a person who made relevant representations in relation to the application desires to contend—

(a) that any variation made ought not to have been made, or

(b) that, when varying the licence, the licensing authority ought not to have modified the conditions of the licence, or ought to have modified them in a different way, under subsection (4)(a) of that section,

he may appeal against the decision.

(4) In sub-paragraph (3) "relevant representations" has the meaning given in section 35(5).

Variation of licence to specify individual as premises supervisor

5 (1) This paragraph applies where an application to vary a premises licence is granted under section 39(2) in a case where a chief officer of police gave a notice under section 37(5) (which was not withdrawn).

(2) The chief officer of police may appeal against the decision to grant the application.

Transfer of licence

6 (1) This paragraph applies where an application to transfer a premises licence is granted under section 44 in a case where a chief officer of police gave a notice under section 42(6) (which was not withdrawn).

(2) The chief officer of police may appeal against the decision to grant the application.

Interim authority notice

7 (1) This paragraph applies where—

(a) an interim authority notice is given in accordance with section 47, and

(b) a chief officer of police gives a notice under section 48(2) (which is not withdrawn).

(2) Where the relevant licensing authority decides to cancel the interim authority notice under subsection (3) of section 48, the person who gave the interim authority notice may appeal against that decision.

(3) Where the relevant licensing authority decides not to cancel the notice under that subsection, the chief officer of police may appeal against that decision.

(4) Where an appeal is brought under sub-paragraph (2), the court to which it is brought may, on such terms as it thinks fit, order the reinstatement of the interim authority notice pending—

(a) the disposal of the appeal, or

(b) the expiry of the interim authority period,

whichever first occurs.

(5) Where the court makes an order under sub-paragraph (4), the premises licence is reinstated from the time the order is made, and section 47 has effect in a case where the appeal is dismissed or abandoned before the end of the interim authority period as if—

(a) the reference in subsection (7)(b) to the end of the interim authority period were a reference to the time when the appeal is dismissed or abandoned, and

(b) the reference in subsection (9)(a) to the interim authority period were a reference to that period disregarding the part of it which falls after that time.

(6) In this paragraph "interim authority period" has the same meaning as in section 47.

Review of premises licence

8 (1) This paragraph applies where an application for a review of a premises licence is decided under section 52.

(2) An appeal may be made against that decision by—

(a) the applicant for the review,

(b) the holder of the premises licence, or

(c) any other person who made relevant representations in relation to the application.

(3) In sub-paragraph (2) "relevant representations" has the meaning given in section 52(7).

General provision about appeals under this Part

9 (1) An appeal under this Part must be made to the magistrates' court for the petty sessions area (or any such area) in which the premises concerned are situated.

(2) An appeal under this Part must be commenced by notice of appeal given by the appellant to the justices' chief executive for the magistrates' court within the period of 21 days beginning with the day on which the appellant was notified by the licensing authority of the decision appealed against.

(3) On an appeal under paragraph 2(3), 3(2)(b), 4(3), 5(2), 6(2) or 8(2)(a) or (c), the holder of the premises licence is to be the respondent in addition to the licensing authority.

(4) On an appeal under paragraph 7(3), the person who gave the interim authority notice is to be the respondent in addition to the licensing authority.

PART 2

CLUB PREMISES CERTIFICATES

Rejection of applications relating to club premises certificates

10 Where a licensing authority—

(a) rejects an application for a club premises certificate under section 72, or

(b) rejects (in whole or in part) an application to vary a club premises certificate under section 85,

the club that made the application may appeal against the decision.

Decision to grant club premises certificate or impose conditions etc.

11 (1) This paragraph applies where a licensing authority grants a club premises certificate under section 72.

(2) The club holding the certificate may appeal against any decision—

(a) to impose conditions on the certificate under subsection (2) or (3)(b) of that section, or

(b) to take any step mentioned in subsection (4)(b) of that section (exclusion of qualifying club activity).

(3) Where a person who made relevant representations in relation to the application desires to contend—

(a) that the certificate ought not to have been granted, or

(b) that, on granting the certificate, the licensing authority ought to have imposed different or additional conditions, or to have taken a step mentioned in subsection (4)(b) of that section,

he may appeal against the decision.

(4) In sub-paragraph (3) "relevant representations" has the meaning given in section 72(7).

Variation of club premises certificate

12 (1) This paragraph applies where an application to vary a club premises certificate is granted (in whole or in part) under section 85.

(2) The club may appeal against any decision to modify the conditions of the certificate under subsection (3)(b) of that section.

(3) Where a person who made relevant representations in relation to the application desires to contend—

(a) that any variation ought not to have been made, or

(b) that, when varying the certificate, the licensing authority ought not to have modified the conditions of the certificate, or ought to have modified them in a different way, under subsection (3)(b) of that section,

he may appeal against the decision.

(4) In sub-paragraph (3) "relevant representations" has the meaning given in section 85(5).

Review of club premises certificate

13 (1) This paragraph applies where an application for a review of a club premises certificate is decided under section 88.

(2) An appeal may be made against that decision by—

(a) the applicant for the review,

(b) the club that holds or held the club premises certificate, or

(c) any other person who made relevant representations in relation to the application.

(3) In sub-paragraph (2) "relevant representations" has the meaning given in section 88(7).

Withdrawal of club premises certificate

14 Where the relevant licensing authority gives notice withdrawing a club premises certificate under section 90, the club which holds or held the certificate may appeal against the decision to withdraw it.

General provision about appeals under this Part

15 (1) An appeal under this Part must be made to the magistrates' court for the petty sessions area (or any such area) in which the premises concerned are situated.

(2) An appeal under this Part must be commenced by notice of appeal given by the appellant to the justices' chief executive for the magistrates' court within the period of 21 days beginning with the day on which the appellant was notified by the licensing authority of the decision appealed against.

(3) On an appeal under paragraph 11(3), 12(3) or 13(2)(a) or (c), the club that holds or held the club premises certificate is to be the respondent in addition to the licensing authority.

PART 3

OTHER APPEALS

Temporary event notices

16 (1) This paragraph applies where—

(a) a temporary event notice is given under section 100, and

(b) a chief officer of police gives an objection notice in accordance with section 104(2).

(2) Where the relevant licensing authority gives a counter notice under section 105(3), the premises user may appeal against that decision.

(3) Where that authority decides not to give such a counter notice, the chief officer of police may appeal against that decision.

(4) An appeal under this paragraph must be made to the magistrates' court for the petty sessions area (or any such area) in which the premises concerned are situated.

(5) An appeal under this paragraph must be commenced by notice of appeal given by the appellant to the justices' chief executive for the magistrates' court within the period of 21 days beginning with the day on which the appellant was notified by the licensing authority of the decision appealed against.

(6) But no appeal may be brought later than five working days before the day on which the event period specified in the temporary event notice begins.

(7) On an appeal under sub-paragraph (3), the premises user is to be the respondent in addition to the licensing authority.

(8) In this paragraph—

"objection notice" has the same meaning as in section 104; and

"relevant licensing authority" has the meaning given in section 99.

Personal licences

17 (1) Where a licensing authority—

(a) rejects an application for the grant of a personal licence under section 120, or

(b) rejects an application for the renewal of a personal licence under section 121,

the applicant may appeal against that decision.

(2) Where a licensing authority grants an application for a personal licence under section 120(7), the chief officer of police who gave the objection notice (within the meaning of section 120(5)) may appeal against that decision.

(3) Where a licensing authority grants an application for the renewal of a personal licence under section 121(6), the chief officer of police who gave the objection notice (within the meaning of section 121(3)) may appeal against that decision.

(4) Where a licensing authority revokes a personal licence under section 124(4), the holder of the licence may appeal against that decision.

(5) Where in a case to which section 124 (convictions coming to light after grant or renewal) applies—

(a) the chief officer of police for the licensing authority's area gives a notice under subsection (3) of that section (and does not later withdraw it), and

(b) the licensing authority decides not to revoke the licence,

the chief officer of police may appeal against the decision.

(6) An appeal under this paragraph must be made to the magistrates' court for a petty sessions area in which the licensing authority's area (or any part of it) is situated.

(7) An appeal under this paragraph must be commenced by notice of appeal given by the appellant to the justices' chief executive for the magistrates' court within the period of 21 days beginning with the day on which the appellant was notified by the licensing authority of the decision appealed against.

(8) On an appeal under sub-paragraph (2), (3) or (5), the holder of the personal licence is to be the respondent in addition to the licensing authority.

(9) Sub-paragraph (10) applies where the holder of a personal licence gives notice of appeal against a decision of a licensing authority to refuse to renew it.

(10) The relevant licensing authority, or the magistrates' court to which the appeal has been made, may, on such conditions as it thinks fit—

(a) order that the licence is to continue in force until the relevant time, if it would otherwise cease to have effect before that time, or

(b) where the licence has already ceased to have effect, order its reinstatement until the relevant time.

(11) In sub-paragraph (10) "the relevant time" means—

(a) the time the appeal is dismissed or abandoned, or

(b) where the appeal is allowed, the time the licence is renewed.

Closure orders

18 (1) This paragraph applies where, on a review of a premises licence under section 167, the relevant licensing authority decides under subsection (5)(b) of that section—

(a) to take any of the steps mentioned in subsection (6) of that section, in relation to a premises licence for those premises, or

(b) not to take any such step.

(2) An appeal may be made against that decision by—

(a) the holder of the premises licence, or

(b) any other person who made relevant representations in relation to the review.

(3) Where an appeal is made under this paragraph against a decision to take any of the steps mentioned in section 167(6)(a) to (d) (modification of licence conditions etc.), the appropriate magistrates' court may in a case within section 168(3) (premises closed when decision taken)—

(a) if the relevant licensing authority has not made an order under section 168(5) (order suspending operation of decision in whole or part), make any order under section 168(5) that could have been made by the relevant licensing authority, or

(b) if the authority has made such an order, cancel it or substitute for it any order which could have been made by the authority under section 168(5).

(4) Where an appeal is made under this paragraph in a case within section 168(6) (premises closed when decision to revoke made to remain closed pending appeal), the appropriate magistrates court may, on such conditions as it thinks fit, order that section 168(7) (premises to remain closed pending appeal) is not to apply to the premises.

(5) An appeal under this paragraph must be commenced by notice of appeal given by the appellant to the justices' chief executive for the magistrates' court within the period of 21 days beginning with the day on which the appellant was notified by the relevant licensing authority of the decision appealed against.

(6) On an appeal under this paragraph by a person other than the holder of the premises licence, that holder is to be the respondent in addition to the licensing authority that made the decision.

(7) In this paragraph—

"appropriate magistrates' court" means the magistrates court for the petty sessions area (or any such area) in which the premises concerned are situated;

"relevant licensing authority" has the same meaning as in Part 3 of this Act; and

"relevant representations" has the meaning given in section 167(9).

SCHEDULE 6

Section 198

MINOR AND CONSEQUENTIAL AMENDMENTS

Universities (Wine Licences) Act 1743 (c. 40)

1 The Universities (Wine Licences) Act 1743 ceases to have effect.

Disorderly Houses Act 1751 (c. 36)

2 The Disorderly Houses Act 1751 does not apply in relation to relevant premises within the meaning of section 159 of the Licensing Act 2003.

Sunday Observance Act 1780 (c. 49)

3 The Sunday Observance Act 1780 ceases to have effect.

Town Police Clauses Act 1847 (c. 89)

4 Section 35 of the Town Police Clauses Act 1847 (harbouring thieves or prostitutes at a public venue) ceases to have effect.

Cambridge Award Act 1856 (c. xvii)

5 The following provisions of the Cambridge Award Act 1856 cease to have effect—

(a) section 9 (revocation of alehouse licence by justice of the peace following complaint by Vice Chancellor of the University), and

(b) section 11 (power to grant wine licence, etc. to remain vested in the Chancellor, Masters and Scholars of the University).

Inebriates Act 1898 (c. 60)

6 In the First Schedule to the Inebriates Act 1898 (offences by reference to which section 6 of the Licensing Act 1902 operates)—

(a) omit the entry relating to section 18 of the Licensing Act 1872 and the entry relating to section 41 of the Refreshment Houses Act 1860, and

(b) after the entries relating to the Merchant Shipping Act 1894 insert—

"Failing to leave licensed premises, etc. when asked to do so.	Licensing Act 2003, s 143.
Entering, or attempting to enter, licensed premises, etc. when asked not to do so."	

Licensing Act 1902 (c. 28)

7 The Licensing Act 1902 is amended as follows.

8 (1) Section 6 (prohibition of sale of alcohol to person declared by the court to be a habitual drunkard) is amended as follows.

(2) For subsection (2) substitute—

"(2) Subsections (2A) to (2C) apply where a court, in pursuance of this Act, orders notice of a conviction to be sent to a police authority.

(2A) The court shall inform the convicted person that the notice is to be sent to a police authority.

(2B) The convicted person commits an offence if, within the three year period, he buys or obtains, or attempts to buy or obtain, alcohol on relevant premises.

(2C) A person to whom subsection (2D) applies commits an offence if, within the three year period, he knowingly—

(a) sells, supplies or distributes alcohol on relevant premises, or

(b) allows the sale, supply or distribution of alcohol on relevant premises,

to, or for consumption by, the convicted person.

(2D) This subsection applies—

(a) to any person who works at the premises in a capacity, whether paid or unpaid, which gives him authority to sell, supply or distribute the alcohol concerned,

(b) in the case of licensed premises, to—

(i) the holder of a premises licence which authorises the sale or supply of alcohol, and

(ii) the designated premises supervisor (if any) under such a licence,

(c) in the case of premises in respect of which a club premises certificate authorising the sale or supply of alcohol has effect, to any member or officer of the club which holds the certificate who at the time the sale, supply or distribution takes place is present on the premises in a capacity which enables him to prevent it, and

(d) in the case of premises which may be used for a permitted temporary activity by virtue of Part 5 of the Licensing Act 2003, the premises user in respect of a temporary event notice authorising the sale or supply of alcohol.

(2E) A person guilty of an offence under this section is liable on summary conviction—

(a) in the case of an offence under subsection (2B), to a fine not exceeding level 1 on the standard scale, and

(b) in the case of an offence under subsection (2C), to a fine not exceeding level 2 on the standard scale."

(3) In subsection (3), for "licensed persons, and secretaries of clubs registered under Part III of this Act," substitute "persons to whom subsection (4) applies".

(4) After that subsection insert—

"(4) This subsection applies to—

(a) the holder of a premises licence which authorises the sale or supply of alcohol,

(b) the designated premises supervisor (if any) under such a licence,

(c) the holder of a club premises certificate authorising the sale or supply of alcohol, and

(d) the premises user in relation to a temporary event notice authorising the sale or supply or alcohol.

(5) In this section—

"alcohol", "club premises certificate", "designated premises supervisor", "licensed premises", "permitted temporary activity", "premises licence", "premises user" and "temporary event notice" have the same meaning as in the Licensing Act 2003,

"relevant premises" means premises which are relevant premises within the meaning of section 159 of that Act and on which alcohol may be lawfully sold or supplied, and

"the three year period", in relation to the convicted person, means the period of three years beginning with the day of the conviction."

9 After section 8 (meaning of "public place") insert—

"8A Interpretation of "licensed premises"

8A For those purposes, "licensed premises" includes—

(a) any licensed premises within the meaning of section 193 of the Licensing Act 2003, and

(b) any premises which may be used for a permitted temporary activity by virtue of Part 5 of that Act."

Celluloid and Cinematograph Film Act 1922 (c. 35)

10 At the end of section 2 of the Celluloid and Cinematograph Film Act 1922 (premises to which the Act does not apply), add "or which may, by virtue of an authorisation (within the meaning of section 136 of the Licensing Act 2003), be used for an exhibition of a film (within the meaning of paragraph 15 of Schedule 1 to that Act)".

Sunday Entertainments Act 1932 (c. 51)

11 The Sunday Entertainments Act 1932 ceases to have effect.

Children and Young Persons Act 1933 (c. 12)

12 The Children and Young Persons Act 1933 is amended as follows.

13 In section 5 (giving alcohol to a child under five) for "intoxicating liquor" substitute "alcohol (within the meaning given by section 191 of the Licensing Act 2003, but disregarding subsection (1)(f) to (i) of that section)".

14 In section 12 (failing to provide for safety of children at entertainments)—

(a) in subsection (3) omit the words from ", and also" to the end,

(b) in subsection (5), for paragraph (a) substitute—

"(a) in the case of a building in respect of which a premises licence authorising the provision of regulated entertainment has effect, be the duty of the relevant licensing authority;", and

(c) after that subsection, insert—

"(5A) For the purposes of this section—

(a) "premises licence" and "the provision of regulated entertainment" have the meaning given by the Licensing Act 2003, and

(b) "the relevant licensing authority", in relation to a building in respect of which a premises licence has effect, means the relevant licensing authority in relation to that building under section 12 of that Act."

15 In section 107 (interpretation), omit the definition of "intoxicating liquor".

Public Health Act 1936 (c. 49)

16 In section 226 of the Public Health Act 1936 (power of local authority to close swimming bath and use it instead for other purposes)—

(a) for subsection (3) substitute—

"(3) Nothing in this section shall authorise the use of a swimming bath or bathing place for the provision of regulated entertainment (within the meaning of the Licensing Act 2003), unless that activity is carried on under and in accordance with an authorisation (within the meaning given in section 136 of that Act).", and

(b) omit subsection (4).

London Building Acts (Amendment) Act 1939 (c. xcvii)

17 In each of the following provisions of the London Building Acts (Amendment) Act 1939, for "the premises are so licensed" substitute "the premises are premises which, by virtue of a premises licence under the Licensing Act 2003, may be used for the supply of alcohol (within the meaning of section 14 of that Act) for consumption on the premises"—

(a) section 11(9)(b) (exemption of licensed premises from provision as to naming of buildings),

(b) paragraph (A) of the proviso to section 13 (offences as to numbering or naming of buildings).

Civic Restaurants Act 1947 (c. 22)

18 In section 1(4) of the Civic Restaurants Act 1947 (civic restaurant authority to be subject to law relating to sale of alcohol), for "the enactments relating to the sale of intoxicating liquor" substitute "the Licensing Act 2003 and any other enactment relating to the sale of intoxicating liquor".

London County Council (General Powers) Act 1947 (c. xlvi)

19 In section 6(1)(b) of the London County Council (General Powers) Act 1947 (saving in connection with the provision of entertainment for enactments relating to the sale

of alcohol), for "any enactment relating to the sale of intoxicating liquor" substitute "the Licensing Act 2003 and any other enactment relating to the sale of intoxicating liquor".

National Parks and Access to the Countryside Act 1949 (c. 97)

20 In each of the following provisions of the National Parks and Countryside Act 1949, for "intoxicating liquor" substitute "alcohol (within the meaning of the Licensing Act 2003)"—

(a) section 12(1)(a) (provision of facilities in National Park),

(b) section 54(2) (provision of facilities along long-distance routes).

Reserve and Auxiliary Forces (Protection of Civil Interests) Act 1951 (c. 65)

21 The Reserve and Auxiliary Forces (Protection of Civil Interests) Act 1951 is amended as follows.

22 In section 14(2)(a) (protection against insecurity of tenure of place of residence), after "premises" insert "in England and Wales which, by virtue of a premises licence under the Licensing Act 2003, may be used for the supply of alcohol (within the meaning of section 14 of that Act) on the premises or in Scotland which are".

23 In section 18(3)(a) (protection against insecurity of tenure in connection with employment), after "premises" insert "in England and Wales which, by virtue of a premises licence under the Licensing Act 2003, may be used for the supply of alcohol (within the meaning of section 14 of that Act) on the premises for consumption on the premises or in Scotland which are".

24 In section 27(1) (renewal of tenancy expiring during period of service), in the second paragraph (c), for the words "licensed for the sale of intoxicating liquor for consumption on the premises" substitute "which, by virtue of a premises licence under the Licensing Act 2003, may be used for the supply of alcohol (within the meaning of section 14 of that Act) for consumption on the premises".

Hypnotism Act 1952 (c. 46)

25 The Hypnotism Act 1952 is amended as follows.

26 (1) Section 1 (inclusion in an entertainment licence of conditions in relation to demonstrations of hypnotism) is amended as follows.

(2) In subsection (1)—

(a) after "any area" insert "in Scotland", and

(b) for "places kept or ordinarily used for public dancing, singing, music or other public entertainment of the like kind" substitute "theatres or other places of public amusement or public entertainment".

(3) Omit subsection (2).

27 In section 2 (requirement for authorisation for demonstration of hypnotism)—

(a) in subsection (1), for the words from "in relation" to the end substitute ", unless—

(a) the controlling authority have authorised that exhibition, demonstration or performance under this section, or

(b) the place is in Scotland and a licence mentioned in section 1 of this Act is in force in relation to it.",

(b) in subsection (1A) for the words from "either at premises" to the end substitute "at premises in Scotland in respect of which a licence under that Act is in force",

(c) after subsection (3) insert—

"(3A) A function conferred by this section on a licensing authority is, for the purposes of section 7 of the Licensing Act 2003 (exercise and delegation by licensing authority of licensing functions), to be treated as a licensing function within the meaning of that Act.", and

(d) for subsection (4) substitute—

"(4) In this section—

"controlling authority" means—

(a) in relation to a place in England and Wales, the licensing authority in whose area the place, or the greater or greatest part of it, is situated, and

(b) in relation to a place in Scotland, the authority having power to grant licences of the kind mentioned in section 1 in that area, and

"licensing authority" has the meaning given by the Licensing Act 2003."

Obscene Publications Act 1959 (c. 66)

28 (1) Section 2 of the Obscene Publications Act 1959 (prohibition of publication of obscene matter) is amended as follows.

(2) In subsections (3A) and (4A), for "a film exhibition" in each place it occurs, substitute "an exhibition of a film".

(3) For subsection (7) substitute—

"(7) In this section, "exhibition of a film" has the meaning given in paragraph 15 of Schedule 1 to the Licensing Act 2003."

Betting, Gaming and Lotteries Act 1963 (c. 2)

29 The Betting, Gaming and Lotteries Act 1963 is amended as follows.

30 In section 10(1B) (conduct of licensed betting offices) for "the provision in a licensed betting office of any facility in respect of which a licence under the Licensing Act 1964 or the Licensing (Scotland) Act 1976 is required" substitute—

"(a) in a licensed betting office in England and Wales, the supply of alcohol (within the meaning of section 14 of the Licensing Act 2003) in circumstances where that supply is a licensable activity (within the meaning of that Act);

(b) in a licensed betting office in Scotland, the provision of any facility in respect of which a licence is required under the Licensing (Scotland) Act 1976".

31 In Schedule 4 (rules for licensed betting offices), in paragraph 10(a), for "intoxicating liquor within the meaning of section 201(1) of the Licensing Act 1964" substitute "alcohol within the meaning of section 191 of the Licensing Act 2003".

Children and Young Persons Act 1963 (c. 37)

32 For section 37(2)(b) of the Children and Young Persons Act 1963 (restriction on performance by child in licensed premises) substitute—

"(b) any performance in premises—

(i) which, by virtue of an authorisation (within the meaning of section 136 of the Licensing Act 2003), may be used for the supply of alcohol (within the meaning of section 14 of that Act), or

(ii) which are licensed premises (within the meaning of the Licensing (Scotland) Act 1976) or in respect of which a club is registered under that Act;".

Offices, Shops and Railway Premises Act 1963 (c. 41)

33 In section 90 of the Offices, Shops and Railway Premises Act 1963 (interpretation), omit the definition of "place of public entertainment".

Greater London Council (General Powers) Act 1966 (c. xxviii)

34 The Greater London Council (General Powers) Act 1966 is amended as follows.

35 In section 21(1) (licensing of public exhibitions, etc.)—

(a) for "intoxicating liquor" substitute "alcohol (within the meaning of the Licensing Act 2003)", and

(b) for "a film exhibition within the meaning of the Cinemas Act 1985" substitute "an exhibition of a film (within the meaning of paragraph 15 of Schedule 1 to the Licensing Act 2003)".

36 In section 22 (application to old buildings of provisions for protection against fire in the London Building Acts (Amendment) Act 1939)—

(a) in subsection (1), for the words from "being in either case" to "for that purpose" substitute "which may lawfully be used for the provision of regulated entertainment (within the meaning of the Licensing Act 2003) only by virtue of an authorisation under that Act", and

(b) in subsection (2), for the words from "where" to "that licence" substitute "where a building, or part of a building, is being used for the provision of regulated entertainment by virtue of a premises licence (under the Licensing Act 2003) granted by a borough council, the Common Council, the Sub-Treasurer of the Inner Temple or the Under-Treasurer of the Middle Temple".

Finance Act 1967 (c. 54)

37 In section 5 of the Finance Act 1967 (no requirement for excise licence)—

(a) in subsection (1), omit paragraph (c), and

(b) in subsection (3), omit "which is registered within the meaning of the Licensing Act 1964 or".

Criminal Appeal Act 1968 (c. 19)

38 The Criminal Appeal Act 1968 is amended as follows.

39 In section 10 (appeal against sentence to Crown Court), at the end of subsection (3)(c) add—

"(viii) an order under section 129 of the Licensing Act 2003 (forfeiture or suspension of personal licence); or".

40 In section 31 (powers of Court of Appeal under Part 1 exercisable by single judge), after subsection (2B) insert—

"(2C) The power of the Court of Appeal, under section 130 of the Licensing Act 2003, to suspend an order under section 129 of that Act may be exercised by a single judge in the same manner as it may be exercised by the Court."

41 In section 44 (powers of Court of Appeal under Part 2 exercisable by single judge), after subsection (2) insert—

"(3) The power of the Court of Appeal, under section 130 of the Licensing Act 2003, to suspend an order under section 129 of that Act may be exercised by a single judge, but where the judge refuses an application to exercise that power the applicant shall be entitled to have the application determined by the Court of Appeal."

42 In section 50 (meaning of "sentence"), at the end of subsection (1) insert "; and

(i) an order under section 129(2) of the Licensing Act 2003 (forfeiture or suspension of personal licence)."

Theatres Act 1968 (c. 54)

43 The Theatres Act 1968 is amended as follows.

44 The following provisions cease to have effect in England and Wales—

(a) section 1(2) (local authority may not impose conditions on nature of plays),

(b) sections 12 to 14 (licensing of premises for public performance of plays),

(c) Schedule 1 (provision about licences to perform plays).

45 In section 15 (warrant to enter theatre where offence suspected)—

(a) in subsection (1)—

(i) paragraph (b) and the word "or" immediately preceding it, and

(ii) the words "or, in a case falling within paragraph (b) above, any police officer or authorised officer of the licensing authority",

cease to have effect in England and Wales,

(b) subsections (2) to (5) cease to have effect in England and Wales, and

(c) subsection (6) is omitted.

46 Section 17 (existing letters patent) ceases to have effect.

47 In section 18(1) (interpretation), in the definition of "licensing authority", omit paragraphs (a), (b) and (bb).

Gaming Act 1968 (c. 65)

48 The Gaming Act 1968 is amended as follows.

49 (1) Section 6 (playing games on premises used for sale of alcohol) is amended as follows.

(2) For subsection (2) substitute—

"(2) This section applies to any premises in England and Wales in respect of which there is in force a premises licence authorising the supply of alcohol for consumption on the premises.

(2A) This section also applies to any premises in Scotland in respect of which a hotel licence or public house licence under the Licensing (Scotland) Act 1976 is in force."

(3) In subsection (3)—

(a) for paragraph (a) substitute—

"(a) of the holder of the licence which has effect in respect of any premises to which this section applies,", and

(b) for "the licensing justices for the licensing district, or, in Scotland, the licensing board for the licensing area, in which the premises are situated" substitute "the relevant licensing authority, or, in Scotland, the licensing board for the licensing area in which the premises are situated,".

(4) In subsection (4)—

(a) for "the licensing justices for the licensing district, or, in Scotland, the licensing board for the licensing area, in which the premises are situated" substitute "the relevant licensing authority, or, in Scotland, the licensing board for the licensing area in which the premises are situated,", and

(b) for "the justices" substitute "the authority".

(5) In subsection (5), for "licensing justices or a licensing board, the justices or board" substitute "a licensing authority or a licensing board, the authority or board".

(6) In subsection (6) —

(a) for "the licensing justices or" substitute "the relevant licensing authority or the",

(b) for paragraph (a) substitute—

"(a) to the holder of the licence,", and

(c) for "the police area" substitute "each police area".

(7) After subsection (7) insert—

"(7A) A function conferred by this section on a licensing authority is, for the purposes of section 7 of the Licensing Act 2003 (exercise and delegation by licensing authority of licensing functions), to be treated as a licensing function within the meaning of that Act."

(8) For subsection (8) substitute—

"(8) In this section—

"licensing area" has the same meaning as in the Licensing (Scotland) Act 1976,

"licensing authority" and "premises licence" have the same meaning as in the Licensing Act 2003,

"relevant licensing authority", in relation to premises in respect of which a premises licence has effect, means the authority determined in relation to those premises in accordance with section 12 of that Act, and

"supply of alcohol" has the meaning given in section 14 of that Act."

50 For section 7(2) (offence to allow child to take part in gaming on licensed premises) substitute—

"(2) Neither the holder of the licence which has effect in respect of premises to which section 6 applies, nor anybody employed by him, may knowingly allow a person under 18 to take part on those premises in gaming to which this Part applies."

51 For section 8(7) (penalty for contravention of section 7(2)) substitute—

"(7) Any person who contravenes section 7(2) is guilty of an offence and—

(a) where the offence is committed in England and Wales, the person is liable on summary conviction to a fine not exceeding level 5 on the standard scale, and

(b) where the offence is committed in Scotland, the provisions of Schedule 5 to the Licensing (Scotland) Act 1976 are to have effect as they have effect in relation to a contravention of section 68(1) of that Act."

52 (1) Schedule 9 (permits in respect of amusement machine premises) is amended as follows.

(2) In paragraph 1 (interpretation), for paragraph (a) substitute—

"(a) in relation to any premises in England and Wales in respect of which there is in force a premises licence authorising the supply of alcohol for consumption on the premises, means the relevant licensing authority in relation to those premises;".

(3) After that paragraph, insert—

"1A A function conferred by this Schedule on a licensing authority is, for the purposes of section 7 of the Licensing Act 2003 (exercise and delegation by licensing authority of licensing functions), to be treated as a licensing function within the meaning of that Act."

(4) In paragraph 10A (condition in case of licensed premises, etc. that amusement machine must be located in a bar), in sub-paragraph (2)(a), for "has the same meaning as in the Licensing Act 1964" substitute "means any place which, by virtue of a premises licence, may be used for the supply of alcohol and which is exclusively or mainly used for the supply and consumption of alcohol".

(5) In paragraph 11—

(a) in sub-paragraphs (2) and (3) (appeals), for "proper officer of" substitute "clerk to", and

(b) omit sub-paragraph (5).

(6) Omit paragraph 14 (payment of indemnity out of central funds).

(7) In paragraph 21 (fees), for "proper officer" substitute "clerk".

(8) For paragraph 23 (interpretation of expressions relating to licensing) substitute—

"23 In this Schedule—

"alcohol", "licensing authority" and "premises licence" have the same meaning as in the Licensing Act 2003;

"hotel licence" and "public house licence" have the same meaning as in Schedule 1 to the Licensing (Scotland) Act 1976;

"relevant licensing authority", in relation to premises in respect of which a premises licence is in force, means the authority determined in relation to those premises in accordance with section 12 of the Licensing Act 2003; and

"supply of alcohol" is to be construed in accordance with section 14 of that Act."

(9) Omit paragraph 24 (proper officer of an appropriate authority).

City of London (Various Powers) Act 1968 (c. xxxvii)

53 For section 5(3) of the City of London (Various Powers) Act 1968 (entitlement of Corporation of London to apply for and hold licence to sell alcohol in arrangements for catering facilities) substitute—

"(3) The Corporation of London or any person appointed by them in that behalf may, subject to section 16 of the Licensing Act 2003, for the purposes of this section apply for and hold a premises licence under that Act for the sale by retail of alcohol within the meaning of that Act."

Finance Act 1970 (c. 24)

54 In section 6(2)(b) of the Finance Act 1970 (Angostura bitters)—

(a) omit ", the Licensing Act 1964", and

(b) for "either of those Acts" substitute "that Act".

Sunday Theatre Act 1972 (c. 26)

55 The Sunday Theatre Act 1972 ceases to have effect.

Local Government Act 1972 (c. 70)

56 The Local Government Act 1972 is amended as follows.

57 In section 78(1) (supplementary provision relating to changes in local government areas), omit the definition of "public body".

58 In section 101 (arrangements for discharge of functions by local authorities), after subsection (14) insert—

"(15) Nothing in this section applies in relation to any function under the Licensing Act 2003 of a licensing authority (within the meaning of that Act)."

59 In section 145(4) (provision of entertainment), for "intoxicating liquor" substitute "alcohol".

60 Section 204 (licensed premises) ceases to have effect.

61 (1) Schedule 12 (meetings and proceedings of local authorities) is amended as follows.

(2) In the following provisions, for "premises licensed for the sale of intoxicating liquor" substitute "premises which at the time of such a meeting may, by virtue of a premises licence or temporary event notice under the Licensing Act 2003, be used for the supply of alcohol (within the meaning of section 14 of that Act)"—

(a) paragraph 10(1) (location of parish council meetings),

(b) paragraph 26(1) (location of community council meetings).

(3) In the following provisions, for "premises licensed for the sale of intoxicating liquor" substitute "premises which at the time of the meeting may, by virtue of a premises licence or temporary event notice under the Licensing Act 2003, be used for the supply of alcohol (within the meaning of section 14 of that Act)"—

(a) paragraph 14(5) (location of parish meetings),

(b) paragraph 32(2) (location of community meetings).

Lotteries and Amusements Act 1976 (c. 32)

62 Schedule 3 to the Lotteries and Amusements Act 1976 (provision about permits for commercial provision of amusements with prizes) is amended as follows.

63 (1) Paragraph 1 (interpretation) is amended as follows.

(2) In sub-paragraph (1), for paragraph (a) substitute—

"(a) in relation to any premises in England and Wales in respect of which there is in force a premises licence authorising the supply of alcohol for consumption on the premises, the relevant licensing authority in relation to those premises;".

(3) In sub-paragraph (2)—

(a) for the definition of "justices' on-licence", "licensing district" and "Part IV licence" substitute—

""alcohol", "licensing authority" and "premises licence" have the same meaning as in the Licensing Act 2003,",

(b) omit the definition of "the proper officer of the authority", and

(c) at the appropriate place, insert—

""relevant licensing authority", in relation to premises in respect of which a premises licence is in force, means the licensing authority in relation to those premises determined in accordance with section 12 of the Licensing Act 2003;", and

""supply of alcohol" has the same meaning as in section 14 of the Licensing Act 2003;".

(4) After that sub-paragraph insert—

"(3) A function conferred by this Schedule on a licensing authority is, for the purposes of section 7 of the Licensing Act 2003 (exercise and delegation by licensing authority of licensing functions), to be treated as a licensing function within the meaning of that Act."

64 In paragraph 8 (appeals)—

(a) in sub-paragraphs (2) and (3), for "proper officer of" substitute "clerk to", and

(b) omit sub-paragraph (4).

65 Omit paragraph 11 (payment of indemnity from central funds).

66 In paragraph 18 (fees), for "proper officer" substitute "clerk".

Rent Act 1977 (c. 42)

67 In section 11 of the Rent Act 1977 (tenancy of licensed premises not to be protected or statutory tenancy), for "premises licensed for the sale of intoxicating liquors" substitute "premises which, by virtue of a premises licence under the Licensing Act 2003, may be used for the supply of alcohol (within the meaning of section 14 of that Act)".

Greater London Council (General Powers) Act 1978 (c. xiii)

68 The Greater London Council (General Powers) Act 1978 is amended as follows.

69 Section 3 (human posing to be treated as entertainment) ceases to have effect.

70 In section 5(4)(a) (definition of "booking office")—

(a) omit sub-paragraph (ii) and the word "or" immediately preceding it, and

(b) for "sub-paragraphs (i) and (ii)" substitute "sub-paragraph (i)".

Alcoholic Liquor Duties Act 1979 (c. 4)

71 The Alcoholic Liquor Duties Act 1979 is amended as follows.

72 In section 4 (interpretation)—

(a) in the definition of "justices' licence" and "justices' on-licence", omit paragraph (a), and

(b) in the definition of "registered club", omit "which is for the time being registered within the meaning of the Licensing Act 1964 or".

73 In section 71 (exception to penalty for misdescribing alcohol as spirits)—

(a) after subsection (4) insert—

"(4A) Nothing in this section as it applies to England and Wales shall apply to any alcohol (within the meaning of the Licensing Act 2003) which is prepared on any premises which may be lawfully used for the supply of alcohol (within the meaning of section 14 of that Act) for immediate consumption there."

(b) in subsection (5)—

(i) omit "England and Wales or",

(ii) omit paragraph (c), and

(iii) for ", in that club or on board that aircraft, vessel or vehicle," substitute "or in that club".

Licensed Premises (Exclusion of Certain Persons) Act 1980 (c. 32)

74 In section 4(1) of the Licensed Premises (Exclusion of Certain Persons) Act 1980 (interpretation), in the definition of "licensed premises" for the words "a justices' on-licence (within the meaning of section 1 of the Licensing Act 1964)" substitute

"a premises licence under the Licensing Act 2003 authorising the supply of alcohol (within the meaning of section 14 of that Act) for consumption on the premises".

Magistrates' Courts Act 1980 (c. 43)

75 In Part 3 of Schedule 6 to the Magistrates' Courts Act 1980 (matters to which provision relating to fees taken by clerks to justices does not apply), paragraphs 3 and 5 are omitted.

Local Government, Planning and Land Act 1980 (c. 65)

76 The Local Government, Planning and Land Act 1980 is amended as follows.

77 Sections 131 and 132 (licensing in new towns) cease to have effect.

78 In section 133 (miscellaneous provision about new towns), in subsection (1), omit the following definitions—

(a) "development corporation",

(b) "the 1964 Act".

79 In section 146 (disposal of land by urban development corporation)—

(a) in subsection (3), for "intoxicating liquor" substitute "alcohol", and

(b) in subsection (6), for ""intoxicating liquor" has the meaning assigned by section 201 of the Licensing Act 1964" substitute ""alcohol" has the meaning given by section 191 of the Licensing Act 2003".

Indecent Displays (Control) Act 1981 (c. 42)

80 In section 1(4) of the Indecent Displays (Control) Act 1981 (exemptions from offence of displaying indecent matter)—

(a) for paragraph (d) substitute—

"(d) included in a performance of a play (within the meaning of paragraph 14(1) of Schedule 1 to the Licensing Act 2003) in England and Wales or of a play (within the meaning of the Theatres Act 1968) in Scotland;", and

(b) in paragraph (e) for "included in a film exhibition as defined in the Cinemas Act 1985" substitute "included in an exhibition of a film, within the meaning of paragraph 15 of Schedule 1 to the Licensing Act 2003, in England and Wales, or a film exhibition, as defined in the Cinemas Act 1985, in Scotland".

New Towns Act 1981 (c. 64)

81 In section 18 of the New Towns Act 1981 (disposal by development corporation of land to occupiers of it before acquisition by corporation), in subsection (3) for the words "intoxicating liquor ("intoxicating liquor" having the meaning given in section 201(1) of the Licensing Act 1964)" substitute "alcohol (within the meaning of section 191 of the Licensing Act 2003)".

Local Government (Miscellaneous Provisions) Act 1982 (c. 30)

82 The Local Government (Miscellaneous Provisions) Act 1982 is amended as follows.

83 The following provisions cease to have effect—

(a) section 1 (licensing of public entertainment outside Greater London),
(b) sections 4 to 6 (controls on take-away food shops),
(c) Schedule 1 (licensing of public entertainment outside Greater London).

84 In section 10(11) (requirement that apparatus to be installed should be provided with cut-off switch disapplied in relation to cinemas) for the words "premises in respect of which a licence under section 1 of the Cinemas Act 1985 is for the time being in force" substitute "premises in respect of which a premises licence under the Licensing Act 2003 has effect authorising the use of the premises for an exhibition of a film, within the meaning of paragraph 15 of Schedule 1 to that Act".

85 (1) Schedule 3 (control of sex establishments) is amended as follows.

(2) In paragraph 3(2) (premises not to be treated as a sex cinema merely because the exhibition of a film there must be authorised by a licence, etc.)—

(a) for paragraph (a) substitute—

"(a) if they may be used for an exhibition of a film (within the meaning of paragraph 15 of Schedule 1 to the Licensing Act 2003) by virtue of an authorisation (within the meaning of section 136 of that Act), of their use in accordance with that authorisation", and

(b) in paragraph (b), for "that Act" substitute "the Cinemas Act 1985".

(3) In paragraph 3A (exemption for theatres and cinemas from provisions about sex encounter establishments) for paragraphs (i) and (ii) of the proviso substitute—

"(i) for the time being, being used for the provision of regulated entertainment (within the meaning of the Licensing Act 2003), in circumstances where that use is authorised under that Act; or

(ii) for the time being, being used for the purposes of late night refreshment (within the meaning of that Act), in circumstances where that use is so authorised; or".

Representation of the People Act 1983 (c. 2)

86 The Representation of the People Act 1983 is amended as follows.

87 In section 185 (interpretation of Part relating to legal proceedings), for the definition of "Licensing Acts" substitute—

"""Licensing Acts" means the Licensing (Scotland) Act 1976 and the Licensing (Northern Ireland) Order 1996 (as that Act or Order may from time to time have effect);".

88 In Schedule 7 (transitional and saving provision), omit paragraph 4.

Video Recordings Act 1984 (c. 39)

89 In section 3(7) of the Video Recordings Act 1984 (exempted supply of video recording)—

(a) before paragraph (a) insert—

"(za) premises in England and Wales which, by virtue of an authorisation within the meaning of section 136 of the Licensing Act 2003, may be used for the exhibition of a film within the meaning of paragraph 15 of Schedule 1 to that Act,", and

(b) in paragraphs (a) and (c) after "premises", and in paragraph (b) after the first "premises", insert "in Scotland".

Building Act 1984 (c. 55)

90 The Building Act 1984 is amended as follows.

91 In section 24(4) (provision of exits in buildings) for paragraph (c) substitute—

"(c) premises in respect of which a club premises certificate has effect under the Licensing Act 2003,".

92 In section 74(2) (exemption for certain premises from requirement for local authority's consent for cellars and rooms below subsoil water level), omit paragraph (a) and the word "or" immediately following it.

Police and Criminal Evidence Act 1984 (c. 60)

93 In Schedule 1A to the Police and Criminal Evidence Act 1984 (arrestable offences) at the end there is inserted—

"26. Licensing Act 2003

26. An offence under section 143(1) of the Licensing Act 2003 (failure to leave licensed premises, etc.)."

Greater London Council (General Powers) Act 1984 (c. xxvii)

94 In section 15(1) of the Greater London Council (General Powers) Act 1984 (exceptions to power of Council to refuse to register sleeping accommodation), at the end insert "; or

(v) a building—

(a) in respect of which there is in force immediately before the appointed day a premises licence under the Licensing Act 2003 authorising the supply of alcohol (within the meaning of section 14 of that Act) for consumption on the premises, and

(b) the use of which for a specified purpose would not contravene the Town and Country Planning Act 1990."

Cinemas Act 1985 (c. 13)

95 The Cinemas Act 1985 ceases to have effect in England and Wales.

Sporting Events (Control of Alcohol etc.) Act 1985 (c. 57)

96 The Sporting Events (Control of Alcohol etc.) Act 1985 is amended as follows.

97 In the following provisions, for "intoxicating liquor" substitute "alcohol"—

(a) section 1(2) and (3) (alcohol on coaches and trains),

(b) section 1A(2) and (3) (alcohol on certain other vehicles),

(c) section 2(1) (alcohol at sports grounds).

98 Omit section 2(1A) (application to private rooms of offence of having alcohol at designated sporting event).

99 The following provisions cease to have effect—

(a) sections 3 and 4 (order about licensing hours in sports grounds),

(b) section 5 (appeal against such an order),

(c) section 5A (restricted periods in relation to possession of alcohol in private rooms at sports grounds),

(d) section 5B (occasional licences at sports grounds),

(e) section 5C (supply of alcohol by clubs at sports grounds),

(f) section 5D (non-retail sales of alcohol during sporting event),

(g) section 6 (closure of bar during sporting event),

(h) the Schedule (procedure for obtaining order about licensing hours in sports grounds).

100 In section 8 (offences)—

(a) in paragraph (b), for ", 2A(1), 3(10), 5B(2), 5C(3), 5D(2) or 6(2)" substitute "or 2A(1)", and

(b) omit paragraphs (d) and (e).

101 In section 9 (interpretation)—

(a) omit subsection (5), and

(b) for subsection (7) substitute—

"(7) An expression used in this Act and in the Licensing Act 2003 has the same meaning in this Act as in that Act."

Housing Act 1985 (c. 68)

102 The Housing Act 1985 is amended as follows.

103 In section 11 (provision of board facilities by local housing authority)—

(a) for subsection (3) substitute—

"(3) Where a premises licence under Part 3 of the Licensing Act 2003 authorises the sale by retail of alcohol in connection with the provision of facilities of the kind mentioned in subsection (1)(a), then, notwithstanding the terms of that licence, it does not have effect so as to authorise the sale by retail of alcohol for consumption otherwise than with a meal.",

(b) in subsection (4) after "the sale of intoxicating liquor" insert "or the sale by retail of alcohol", and

(c) after that subsection insert—

"(5) An expression used in this section and in the Licensing Act 2003 has the same meaning in this section as in that Act."

104 In Schedule 1 (tenancies which are not secure tenancies), in paragraph 9, for "premises licensed for the sale of intoxicating liquor" substitute "premises which, by virtue of a premises licence under the Licensing Act 2003, may be used for the supply of alcohol (within the meaning of section 14 of that Act)".

Sex Discrimination Act 1986 (c. 59)

105 Section 5 of the Sex Discrimination Act 1986 (discrimination required by public entertainment licence) ceases to have effect.

Fire Safety and Safety of Places of Sport Act 1987 (c. 27)

106 After section 33(2) of the Fire Safety and Safety of Places of Sport Act 1987 (requirements of safety certificate to take precedence over conflicting conditions imposed in licence, etc.) insert—

"(2A) For the purposes of subsection (2)—

(a) "the licensing of premises" includes the granting of a premises licence or club premises certificate under the Licensing Act 2003, and

(b) "licence" is to be construed accordingly."

Norfolk and Suffolk Broads Act 1988 (c. 4)

107 In paragraph 40(1) of Schedule 3 to the Norfolk and Suffolk Broads Act 1988 (provision of facilities by Broads Authority), in paragraph (b) for "intoxicating liquor" substitute "alcohol (within the meaning of the Licensing Act 2003)".

Housing Act 1988 (c. 50)

108 In Schedule 1 to the Housing Act 1988 (tenancies which cannot be assured tenancies), in paragraph 5, for "premises licensed for the sale of intoxicating liquors" substitute "premises which, by virtue of a premises licence under the Licensing Act 2003, may be used for the supply of alcohol (within the meaning of section 14 of that Act)".

Town and Country Planning Act 1990 (c. 8)

109 Section 334 of the Town and Country Planning Act 1990 (licensing planning areas) ceases to have effect.

Sunday Trading Act 1994 (c. 20)

110 (1) Schedule 1 to the Sunday Trading Act 1994 (restrictions on Sunday opening of large shops) is amended as follows.

(2) In paragraph 1—

(a) for the definition of "intoxicating liquor" substitute—

""alcohol" has the same meaning as in the Licensing Act 2003,", and

(b) in paragraph (a) of the definition of "sale of goods", for "intoxicating liquor" substitute "alcohol".

(3) In paragraph 3(1)(b) for "intoxicating liquor" substitute "alcohol".

Criminal Justice and Public Order Act 1994 (c. 33)

111 In section 63 of the Criminal Justice and Public Order Act 1994 (power to remove persons attending raves, etc.), for subsection (9)(a) substitute—

"(a) in England and Wales, to a gathering in relation to a licensable activity within section 1(1)(c) of the Licensing Act 2003 (provision of certain forms of entertainment) carried on under and in accordance with an authorisation within the meaning of section 136 of that Act;".

Deregulation and Contracting Out Act 1994 (c. 40)

112 Section 21 of the Deregulation and Contracting Out Act 1994 (Sunday Observance Act 1780 not to apply to sporting events) ceases to have effect.

London Local Authorities Act 1995 (c. x)

113 In section 14 of the London Local Authorities Act 1995 (interpretation of Part relating to near beer premises), in the definition of "near beer premises"—

(a) for "intoxicating liquor is provided exemption or saving from the provisions of the Act of 1964 by virtue of section 199 of that Act" substitute "alcohol is not a licensable activity under or by virtue of section 173 of the Licensing Act 2003",

(b) for paragraph (A) substitute—

"(A) a premises licence under Part 3 of that Act which authorises the supply of alcohol (within the meaning of section 14 of that Act) for consumption on the premises;",

(c) in paragraph (B)—

(i) omit "Schedule 12 to the London Government Act 1963," and "or the Private Places of Entertainment (Licensing) Act 1967", and

(ii) at the end insert "or a premises licence granted under Part 3 of the Licensing Act 2003 which authorises the provision of any form of regulated entertainment (within the meaning of Schedule 1 to that Act)",

(d) omit paragraphs (C) to (E),

(e) for paragraphs (F) and (G) substitute—

"(F) a temporary event notice under the Licensing Act 2003, by virtue of which the premises may be used for the supply of alcohol (within the meaning of section 14 of that Act);",

(f) for the words from "during the hours" to "licence:" substitute "during the hours permitted by such licence or notice:", and

(g) for "such licence; and" substitute "such licence or notice; and".

Employment Rights Act 1996 (c. 18)

114 In section 232(7) of the Employment Rights Act 1996 (definition of "catering business")—

(a) in paragraph (a) for "intoxicating liquor" substitute "alcohol", and

(b) for ""intoxicating liquor" has the same meaning as in the Licensing Act 1964" substitute ""alcohol" has the same meaning as in the Licensing Act 2003".

Confiscation of Alcohol (Young Persons) Act 1997 (c. 33)

115 (1) Section 1 of the Confiscation of Alcohol (Young Persons) Act 1997 (confiscation of alcohol) is amended as follows.

(2) In subsection (1)—

(a) for "intoxicating liquor", in each place it occurs, substitute "alcohol",

(b) in paragraph (b) for "liquor" substitute "alcohol", and

(c) for "such liquor" substitute "alcohol".

(3) For subsection (7) substitute—

"(7) In this section—

"alcohol"—

(a) in relation to England and Wales, has the same meaning as in the Licensing Act 2003;

(b) in relation to Northern Ireland, has the same meaning as "intoxicating liquor" in the Licensing (Northern Ireland) Order 1996; and

"licensed premises"—

(a) in relation to England and Wales, means premises which may by virtue of Part 3 or Part 5 of the Licensing Act 2003 (premises licence; permitted temporary activity) be used for the supply of alcohol within the meaning of section 14 of that Act;

(b) in relation to Northern Ireland, has the same meaning as in the Licensing (Northern Ireland) Order 1996."

Police Act 1997 (c. 50)

116 In section 115(5) of the Police Act 1997 (enhanced criminal record certificates), after paragraph (d) insert—

"(da) a personal licence under the Licensing Act 2003;".

London Local Authorities Act 2000 (c. vii)

117 In section 32 of the London Local Authorities Act 2000 (interpretation of provisions about the licensing of buskers), in the definition of "busking", for paragraph (b) substitute—

"(b) under and in accordance with a premises licence under Part 3 of the Licensing Act 2003, or a temporary event notice having effect under Part 5 of that Act, which authorises the provision of regulated entertainment (within paragraph 2(1)(e) to (h) or 3(2) of Schedule 1 to that Act (music and dancing));".

Private Security Industry Act 2001 (c. 12)

118 (1) Paragraph 8 of Schedule 2 to the Private Security Industry Act 2001 (door supervisors etc. for licensed premises) is amended as follows.

(2) In sub-paragraph (2), for paragraphs (a) to (d) substitute—

"(a) any premises in respect of which a premises licence or temporary event notice has effect under the Licensing Act 2003 to authorise the supply of alcohol (within the meaning of section 14 of that Act) for consumption on the premises;

(b) any premises in respect of which a premises licence or temporary event notice has effect under that Act to authorise the provision of regulated entertainment;".

(3) For sub-paragraph (3) substitute—

"(3) For the purposes of this paragraph, premises are not licensed premises—

(a) if there is in force in respect of the premises a premises licence which authorises regulated entertainment within paragraph 2(1)(a) or (b) of Schedule 1 to the Licensing Act 2003 (plays and films);

(b) in relation to any occasion on which the premises are being used—

(i) exclusively for the purposes of a club which holds a club premises certificate in respect of the premises, or

(ii) for regulated entertainment of the kind mentioned in paragraph (a), in circumstances where that use is a permitted temporary activity by virtue of Part 5 of that Act;

(c) in relation to any occasion on which a licence is in force in respect of the premises under the Gaming Act 1968 (c. 65) and the premises are being used wholly or mainly for the purposes of gaming to which Part 2 of that Act applies; or

(d) in relation to any such other occasion as may be prescribed for the purposes of this sub-paragraph."

(4) After sub-paragraph (5) insert—

"(6) Sub-paragraphs (2)(a) and (b) and (3)(a) and (b) are to be construed in accordance with the Licensing Act 2003."

Criminal Justice and Police Act 2001 (c. 16)

119 The Criminal Justice and Police Act 2001 is amended as follows.

120 In section 1(1) (offences leading to penalties on the spot), at the end of the Table insert—

"Section 149(4) of the Licensing Act 2003	Buying or attempting to buy alcohol for consumption on licensed premises, etc. by child"

121 In section 12 (alcohol consumption in designated public place)—

(a) in subsections (1) and (2), for "intoxicating liquor", in each place it occurs, substitute "alcohol", and

(b) in subsection (2) for "such liquor" substitute "alcohol".

122 In section 13 (designated public places), in subsection (2) for "intoxicating liquor" substitute "alcohol".

123 (1) Section 14 (places which are not designated public places) is amended as follows.

(2) In subsection (1)—

(a) for paragraphs (a) to (d) substitute—

"(a) premises in respect of which a premises licence or club premises certificate, within the meaning of the Licensing Act 2003, has effect;

(b) a place within the curtilage of premises within paragraph (a);

(c) premises which by virtue of Part 5 of the Licensing Act 2003 may for the time being be used for the supply of alcohol or which, by virtue of that Part, could have been so used within the last 20 minutes;", and

(b) in paragraph (e), for "intoxicating liquor" substitute "alcohol".

(3) Omit subsection (2).

124 In section 15(1)(a) (byelaw prohibiting consumption of alcohol), for "intoxicating liquor" substitute "alcohol".

125 In section 16(1) (interpretation of sections 12 to 15)—

(a) before the definition of "designated public place" insert—

"""alcohol" has the same meaning as in the Licensing Act 2003;",

(b) omit the definition of "intoxicating liquor", and the word "and" immediately following it, and

(c) after the definition of "public place" insert "; and

"supply of alcohol" has the meaning given by section 14 of the Licensing Act 2003".

126 In each of the following provisions, for "unlicensed sale of intoxicating liquor" substitute "unauthorised sale of alcohol"—

(a) section 19(1) and (2) (service of closure notice by constable or local authority),

(b) section 20(3)(a) (no application for closure order where unauthorised sale of alcohol has ceased),

(c) section 21(1)(b) and (2)(b) (closure order),

(d) section 27(6) (fixing notice on premises where personal service cannot be effected).

127 In section 28 (interpretation of provisions relating to closure of unlicensed premises) —

(a) before the definition of "closure notice" insert—

"""alcohol" has the same meaning as in the Licensing Act 2003;",

(b) omit the definition of "intoxicating liquor", and

(c) for the definition of "unlicensed sale" substitute—

"""unauthorised sale", in relation to any alcohol, means any supply of the alcohol (within the meaning of section 14 of the Licensing Act 2003) which—

(a) is a licensable activity within the meaning of that Act, but

(b) is made otherwise than under and in accordance with an authorisation (within the meaning of section 136 of that Act)."

128 In Schedule 1 (powers of seizure)—

(a) at the end of Part 1 insert—

"74. Licensing Act 2003

74. The power of seizure conferred by section 90 of the Licensing Act 2003 (seizure of documents relating to club).", and

(b) at the end of Part 3 insert—

"110. Licensing Act 2003

110. The power of seizure conferred by section 90 of the Licensing Act 2003 (seizure of documents relating to club)."

SCHEDULE 7

Section 199

REPEALS

Short title and chapter	*Extent of repeal*
Universities (Wine Licences) Act 1743 (c. 40)	The whole Act.
Sunday Observance Act 1780 (21 Geo. 3 c. 49)	The whole Act.
Metropolitan Police Act 1839 (c. 47)	Section 41.
Town Police Clauses Act 1847 (c. 89)	Section 35.
Cambridge Award Act 1856 (c. xvii)	Sections 9 and 11.
Inebriates Act 1898 (c. 60)	In the First Schedule— the entry relating to section 18 of the Licensing Act 1872, and the entry relating to section 41 of the Refreshment Houses Act 1860.
Sunday Entertainments Act 1932 (c. 51)	The whole Act.
Children and Young Persons Act 1933 (c. 12)	In section 12(3), the words from ", and also" to the end.
	In section 107, the definition of "intoxicating liquor".
Public Health Act 1936 (c. 49)	Section 226(4).
Common Informers Act 1951 (c. 39)	In the Schedule— the entry relating to section 11 of the Universities (Wine Licences) Act 1743, and

Short title and chapter	*Extent of repeal*
	the entry relating to the Sunday Observance Act 1780.
Hypnotism Act 1952 (c. 46)	Section 1(2).
London Government Act 1963 (c. 33)	Section 52(3).
	Schedule 12.
Offices, Shops and Railway Premises Act 1963 (c. 41)	In section 90, the definition of "place of public entertainment".
Licensing Act 1964 (c. 26)	The whole Act.
Administration of Justice Act 1964 (c. 42)	In Schedule 3, paragraph 31.
Refreshment Houses Act 1964 (c. 88)	The whole Act.
Private Places of Entertainment (Licensing) Act 1967 (c. 19)	The whole Act.
Licensing (Amendment) Act 1967 (c. 51)	The whole Act.
Finance Act 1967 (c. 54)	In section 5— in subsection (1),the words "; and accordingly as from that date—" and paragraphs (c) and (e), and in subsection (3), the words "which is registered within the meaning of the Licensing Act 1964 or".
	Section 45(4).
	Schedule 7.
Theatres Act 1968 (c. 54)	Section 15(6).
	Section 17.
	In section 18(1), in the definition of "licensing authority", paragraphs (a), (b) and (bb).
	In Schedule 2— the entries relating to the Licensing Act 1964, and the entry relating to the Private Places of Entertainment (Licensing) Act 1967.
Gaming Act 1968 (c. 65)	In Schedule 9— paragraph 11(5), paragraph 14, and paragraph 24.
	In Schedule 11, in Part 3, the entries relating to the Licensing Act 1964.
Greater London Council (General Powers) Act 1968 (c.xxxix)	Sections 47 to 55.

Short title and chapter	*Extent of repeal*
Late Night Refreshment Houses Act 1969 (c. 53)	The whole Act.
Finance Act 1970 (c. 24)	In section 6(2)(b), the words ", the Licensing Act 1964".
Courts Act 1971 (c. 23)	In Schedule 6, paragraphs 7 and 13.
	In Schedule 8, paragraph 42.
	In Schedule 9, in Part 1, the entries relating to— the London Government Act 1963, the Licensing Act 1964, the Private Places of Entertainment (Licensing) Act 1967, the Theatres Act 1968, and the Late Night Refreshment Houses Act 1969.
Sunday Theatre Act 1972 (c. 26)	The whole Act.
Local Government Act 1972 (c. 70)	In section 78(1), the definition of "public body".
	Section 204.
	In Schedule 25, paragraphs 1 to 9.
Local Government Act 1974 (c. 7)	In Schedule 6, paragraph 24.
Licensing (Amendment) Act 1976 (c. 18)	The whole Act.
Lotteries and Amusements Act 1976 (c. 32)	In Schedule 3— in paragraph 1(2), the definition of "the proper officer of the authority", and paragraphs 8(4) and 11.
Licensing (Scotland) Act 1976 (c. 66)	In Schedule 7, paragraphs 9(a), (b), (d) and (f), 10, 11 and 12.
Greater London Council (General Powers) Act 1976 (c. xxvi)	Sections 5 to 8.
Licensing (Amendment) Act 1977 (c. 26)	The whole Act.
Greater London Council (General Powers) Act 1978 (c. xiii)	Sections 3 and 4.
	Section 5(4)(a)(ii) and the word "or" immediately preceding it.
Customs and Excise Management Act 1979 (c. 2)	In Schedule 4, in paragraph 12, in the Table, the entry relating to the Licensing Act 1964.
Alcoholic Liquor Duties Act 1979 (c. 4)	In section 4— in the definition of "justices' licence" and "justices' on-licence", paragraph (a), and in the definition of "registered club", the words "which is for the time being

Short title and chapter	Extent of repeal
	registered within the meaning of the Licensing Act 1964 or".
	In section 71(5)— the words "England and Wales or", and paragraph (c).
	In Schedule 3, paragraph 5.
Greater London Council (General Powers) Act 1979 (c. xxiii)	Section 3.
Licensing (Amendment) Act 1980 (c. 40)	The whole Act.
Magistrates' Courts Act 1980 (c. 43)	In Schedule 6, in Part 3, paragraphs 3 and 5.
	In Schedule 7, paragraphs 45 to 48 and 50.
Local Government, Planning and Land Act 1980 (c. 65)	Sections 131 and 132.
	In section 133(1), the definitions of "development corporation" and "the 1964 Act".
Highways Act 1980 (c. 66)	In Schedule 24, paragraph 12.
Finance Act 1981 (c. 35)	In Schedule 8, paragraphs 24 and 25.
Licensing (Amendment) Act 1981 (c. 40)	The whole Act.
Supreme Court Act 1981 (c. 54)	In section 28(2)(b), the words "the Licensing Act 1964,".
New Towns Act 1981 (c. 64)	In Schedule 2, paragraph 2.
	In Schedule 12, paragraphs 1 and 29(a)(i).
Local Government (Miscellaneous Provisions) Act 1982 (c. 30)	Section 1.
	Sections 4 to 7.
	Schedule 1.
	In Schedule 2, paragraphs 1 to 6.
Greater London Council (General Powers) Act 1982 (c. i)	Section 7.
Representation of the People Act 1983 (c. 2)	In Schedule 7, paragraph 4.
	In Schedule 8, paragraphs 7 to 10.
Licensing (Occasional Permissions) Act 1983 (c. 24)	The whole Act.
Building Act 1984 (c. 55)	In section 74(2), paragraph (a) and the word "or" immediately following it.
Greater London Council (General Powers) Act 1984 (c.xxvii)	Section 4(1) and (3).
	Sections 19 to 22.
Cinemas Act 1985 (c. 13)	Section 3(1A).
	Section 9.

Short title and chapter	Extent of repeal
	Sections 17 and 18.
	In section 19(3), paragraph (a) and the word "or" immediately following it.
	In Schedule 2, paragraphs 2, 3, 6, 7, 8, 14, 15 and 16(a) and the word "and" immediately following it.
Licensing (Amendment) Act 1985 (c. 40)	The whole Act.
Local Government Act 1985 (c. 51)	In Schedule 8— paragraph 1(1), in paragraph 1(3), the words following paragraph (c), and paragraphs 2 to 5.
Sporting Events (Control of Alcohol etc.) Act 1985 (c. 57)	Section 2(1A).
	Sections 3 to 6.
	Section 8(d) and (e).
	Section 9(5).
	The Schedule.
Insolvency Act 1985 (c. 65)	In Schedule 8, paragraph 12.
Insolvency Act 1986 (c. 45)	In Schedule 14, the entries relating to the Licensing Act 1964.
Sex Discrimination Act 1986 (c. 59)	Section 5.
Public Order Act 1986 (c. 64)	In Schedule 1, paragraphs 4, 5, 7(5) and 8.
Greater London Council (General Powers) Act 1986 (c. iv)	Section 3.
Fire Safety and Safety of Places of Sport Act 1987 (c. 27)	Sections 42, 43, 45 and 46.
	Schedule 3.
	In Schedule 5— in paragraph 1, the definition of "the 1963 Act" and the definition of "the 1982 Act" and the word "and" immediately preceding it, and paragraphs 8 to 10.
Licensing Act 1988 (c. 17)	The whole Act.
Licensing (Retail Sales) Act 1988 (c. 25)	The whole Act.
Licensing (Amendment) Act 1989 (c. 20)	The whole Act.
Employment Act 1989 (c. 38)	In Schedule 6, paragraph 30.
Town and Country Planning Act 1990 (c. 8)	Section 334.
Entertainments (Increased Penalties) Act 1990 (c. 20)	Section 1.

Short title and chapter	*Extent of repeal*
Licensing (Low Alcohol Drinks) Act 1990 (c. 21)	Section 1.
Broadcasting Act 1990 (c. 42)	In Schedule 20, paragraphs 7 and 8.
London Local Authorities Act 1990 (c. vii)	Sections 4 to 17, 19 and 20.
London Local Authorities (No. 2) Act 1990 (c. xxx)	Section 6.
Finance Act 1991 (c. 31)	In Schedule 2, in paragraph 1, the words ", the Licensing Act 1964".
London Local Authorities Act 1991 (c. xiii)	Sections 18 to 21.
Sporting Events (Control of Alcohol etc.) (Amendment) Act 1992 (c. 57)	The whole Act.
Charities Act 1993 (c. 10)	In Schedule 6, paragraph 27.
Local Government (Wales) Act 1994 (c. 19)	In Schedule 2, paragraph 2.
	In Schedule 15, paragraph 41.
	In Schedule 16, paragraphs 22, 29, 32, 36, 69 and 73.
Coal Industry Act 1994 (c. 21)	In Schedule 9, paragraph 8.
Criminal Justice and Public Order Act 1994 (c. 33)	In section 63— in subsection (10), the definitions of "entertainment licence" and "local authority", and subsection (11).
Deregulation and Contracting Out Act 1994 (c. 40)	Section 18(1).
	Section 19.
	Section 21.
	Schedule 7.
	In Schedule 11, paragraph 1.
London Local Authorities Act 1994 (c. xii)	Section 5.
Licensing (Sunday Hours) Act 1995 (c. 33)	The whole Act.
London Local Authorities Act 1995 (c. x)	In section 14— in paragraph (B), the words "Schedule 12 to the London Government Act 1963," and "or the Private Places of Entertainment (Licensing) Act 1967", and paragraphs (C) to (E).
	Section 28.
	Sections 45 and 46.
London Local Authorities Act 1996 (c. ix)	Sections 20 to 23.

Short title and chapter	*Extent of repeal*
Justices of the Peace Act 1997 (c. 25)	In Schedule 4, in paragraph 17(3), the words "', other than any duties as secretary to a licensing planning committee under Part VII of the Licensing Act 1964".
Confiscation of Alcohol (Young Persons) Act 1997 (c. 33)	In section 1(1), the words "(other than a sealed container)".
Public Entertainments Licences (Drug Misuse) Act 1997 (c. 49)	The whole Act.
Access to Justice Act 1999 (c. 22)	In Schedule 10, paragraphs 23 to 29 and 31.
	In Schedule 11, paragraph 17.
	In Schedule 13, paragraphs 36 to 56, 61, 62, 87, 124 and 132.
Greater London Authority Act 1999 (c. 29)	In Schedule 29, paragraphs 6, 67, 70 and 71.
Licensing (Young Persons) Act 2000 (c. 30)	The whole Act.
Freedom of Information Act 2000 (c. 36)	In Schedule 1, paragraph 17.
London Local Authorities Act 2000 (c. vii)	Sections 22 to 26.
	Schedule 1.
Criminal Justice and Police Act 2001 (c. 16)	In section 1(1), in the Table, the entry relating to section 169C(3) of the Licensing Act 1964.
	In section 12(2)(b), the words "(other than a sealed container)".
	Section 14(2).
	In section 16(1), the definition of "intoxicating liquor" and the word "and" immediately following it.
	Sections 17 and 18.
	In section 28, the definition of "intoxicating liquor".
	Sections 30 to 32.
	In Schedule 1, paragraphs 7 and 90.

SCHEDULE 8

Section 200

TRANSITIONAL PROVISION ETC.

PART 1

PREMISES LICENCES

Introductory

1 (1) In this Part—

"canteen licence" has the same meaning as in section 148 of the 1964 Act (licences for seamen's canteens);

"children's certificate" has the same meaning as in section 168A of that Act;

"existing licence" means—

(a) a justices' licence,

(b) a canteen licence,

(c) a licence under Schedule 12 to the London Government Act 1963 (c. 33) (licensing of public entertainment in Greater London),

(d) a licence under the Private Places of Entertainment (Licensing) Act 1967 (c. 19),

(e) a licence under the Theatres Act 1968 (c. 54),

(f) a licence under the Late Night Refreshment Houses Act 1969 (c. 53),

(g) a licence under Schedule 1 to the Local Government (Miscellaneous Provisions) Act 1982 (c. 30) (licensing of public entertainments outside Greater London),

(h) a licence under section 1 of the Cinemas Act 1985 (c. 13), or

(i) a licence under Part 2 of the London Local Authorities Act 1990 (c.vii) (night cafe licensing);

"existing licensable activities", under an existing licence, are—

(a) the licensable activities authorised by the licence, and

(b) any other licensable activities which may be carried on, at the premises in respect of which the licence has effect, by virtue of the existence of the licence (see sub-paragraph (2));

"first appointed day" means such day as may be specified as the first appointed day for the purposes of this Part;

"new licence" has the meaning given in paragraph 5(1);

"relevant existing licence", in relation to an application under paragraph 2, means an existing licence to which the application relates;

"relevant licensing authority" has the same meaning as in Part 3 of this Act (premises licences);

"second appointed day" means such day as may be specified as the second appointed day for the purposes of this Part; and

"supply of alcohol" means—

(a) sale by retail of alcohol, or

(b) supply of alcohol by or on behalf of a club to, or to the order of, a member of the club.

(2) In determining, for the purposes of paragraph (b) of the definition of "existing licensable activities", the other licensable activities which may be carried on by virtue of a licence—

(a) section 182 of the 1964 Act (relaxation of law relating to music and dancing licences) is to be disregarded so far as it relates to public entertainment by way of music and singing provided by not more than two performers, and

(b) in the case of an existing licence granted under the Theatres Act 1968 (c. 54), the reference in that paragraph to the licence is to be read as including a reference to any notice in force under section 199(c) of the 1964 Act (notice of intention to sell alcohol by retail at licensed theatre premises) in relation to that licence.

(3) In the application of section 12 (relevant licensing authority in Part 3 of this Act) for the purposes of this Part, the reference in subsection (4)(a) of that section to an applicant for a premises licence is to be read as a reference to an applicant under paragraph 2 for the grant of a licence under paragraph 4.

Application for conversion of existing licence

2 (1) This paragraph applies where, in respect of any premises, one or more existing licences have effect on the first appointed day.

(2) A person may, within the period of six months beginning with the first appointed day, apply to the relevant licensing authority for the grant of a licence under paragraph 4 to succeed one or more of those existing licences.

(3) But an application may be made under this paragraph in respect of an existing licence only if—

(a) it is held by the applicant, or

(b) the holder of the licence consents to the application being made.

(4) An application under this paragraph must specify—

(a) the existing licensable activities under the relevant existing licence or, if there is more than one, the relevant existing licences,

(b) if any relevant existing licence authorises the supply of alcohol, specified information about the person whom the applicant wishes to be the premises supervisor under the licence granted under paragraph 4, and

(c) such other information as may be specified.

(5) The application must also be in the specified form and accompanied by—

(a) the relevant documents, and

(b) the specified fee.

(6) The relevant documents are—

(a) the relevant existing licence or, if there is more than one, each of them (or a certified copy of the licence or licences in question),

(b) a plan in the specified form of the premises to which the relevant existing licence or licences relate,

(c) if any relevant existing licence authorises the supply of alcohol, any children's certificate in force in respect of the premises (or a certified copy of any such certificate),

(d) a form of consent in the specified form, given by the individual (if any) named in the application in accordance with sub-paragraph (4)(b),

(e) a form of consent in the specified form, given by any person who is required to consent to the application under sub-paragraph (3), and

(f) such other documents as may be specified.

(7) In this paragraph any reference to a certified copy of a document is a reference to a copy of that document certified to be a true copy—

(a) in the case of a justices' licence, children's certificate or canteen licence, by the chief executive of the licensing justices for the licensing district in which the premises are situated,

(b) in any other case, by the chief executive of the local authority which issued the licence,

(c) by a solicitor or notary, or

(d) by a person of a specified description.

(8) A document which purports to be a certified copy of an existing licence or children's certificate is to be taken to be such a copy unless the contrary is shown.

Police consultation

3 (1) Where a person makes an application under paragraph 2, he must give a copy of the application (and any documents which accompanied it) to the chief officer of police for the police area (or each police area) in which the premises are situated no later than 48 hours after the application is made.

(2) Where—

(a) an appeal is pending against a decision to revoke, or to reject an application for the renewal of, the relevant existing licence or, if there is more than one such licence, a relevant existing licence, and

(b) a chief officer of police who has received a copy of the application under sub-paragraph (1) is satisfied that converting that existing licence in accordance with this Part would undermine the crime prevention objective,

he must give the relevant licensing authority and the applicant a notice to that effect.

(3) Where a chief officer of police who has received a copy of an application under sub-paragraph (1) is satisfied that, because of a material change in circumstances since the relevant time, converting the relevant existing licence or, if there is more than one such licence, a relevant existing licence in accordance with this Part would undermine the crime prevention objective, he must give the relevant licensing authority and the applicant a notice to that effect.

(4) For this purpose "relevant time" means the time when the relevant existing licence was granted or, if it has been renewed, the last time it was renewed.

(5) The chief officer of police may not give a notice under sub-paragraph (2) or (3) after the end of the period of 28 days beginning with the day on which he received a copy of the application under sub-paragraph (1).

Determination of application

4 (1) This paragraph applies where an application is made in accordance with paragraph 2 and the applicant complies with paragraph 3(1).

(2) Subject to sub-paragraphs (3) and (5), the relevant licensing authority must grant the application.

(3) Where a notice is given under paragraph 3(2) or (3) in respect of an existing licence (and not withdrawn), the authority must—

(a) hold a hearing to consider it, unless the authority, the applicant and the chief officer of police who gave the notice agree that a hearing is unnecessary, and

(b) having regard to the notice—

(i) in a case where the application relates only to that licence, reject the application, and

(ii) in any other case, reject the application to the extent that it relates to that licence,

if it considers it necessary for the promotion of the crime prevention objective to do so.

(4) If the relevant licensing authority fails to determine the application within the period of two months beginning with the day on which it received it, then, subject to sub-paragraph (5), the application is to be treated as granted by the authority under this paragraph.

(5) An application must not be granted (and is not to be treated as granted under sub-paragraph (4))—

(a) if the relevant existing licence has or, if there is more than one, all the relevant existing licences have ceased to be held by the applicant before the relevant time, or

(b) where there is more than one relevant existing licence (but paragraph (a) does not apply), to the extent that the application relates to an existing licence which has ceased to be held by the applicant before the relevant time.

(6) For the purposes of sub-paragraph (5)—

(a) where, for the purposes of paragraph 2(3)(b) a person has consented to an application being made in respect of a relevant existing licence, sub-paragraph (5)(a) and (b) applies in relation to that licence as if the reference to the applicant were a reference to—

(i) that person, or

(ii) any other person to whom the existing licence has been transferred and who has given his consent for the purposes of this paragraph, and

(b) "the relevant time" is the time of the determination of the application or, in a case within sub-paragraph (4), the end of the period mentioned in that sub-paragraph.

(7) Section 10 applies as if the relevant licensing authority's functions under sub-paragraph (3) were included in the list of functions in subsection (4) of that section (functions which cannot be delegated to an officer of the licensing authority).

Notification of determination and issue of new licence

5 (1) Where an application is granted (in whole or in part) under paragraph 4, the relevant licensing authority must forthwith—

(a) give the applicant a notice to that effect, and

(b) issue the applicant with—

(i) a licence in respect of the premises (a "new licence") in accordance with paragraph 6, and

(ii) a summary of the new licence.

(2) Where an application is rejected (in whole or in part) under paragraph 4, the relevant licensing authority must forthwith give the applicant a notice to that effect stating the authority's reasons for its decision to reject the application.

(3) The relevant licensing authority must give a copy of any notice it gives under sub-paragraph (1) or (2) to the chief officer of police for the police area (or each police area) in which the premises to which the notice relates are situated.

The new licence

6 (1) This paragraph applies where a new licence is granted under paragraph 4 in respect of one or more existing licences.

(2) Where an application under paragraph 2 is granted in part only, any relevant existing licence in respect of which the application was rejected is to be disregarded for the purposes of the following provisions of this paragraph.

(3) The new licence is to be treated as if it were a premises licence (see section 11), and sections 19, 20 and 21 (mandatory conditions for premises licences) apply in relation to it accordingly.

(4) The new licence takes effect on the second appointed day.

(5) The new licence must authorise the premises in question to be used for the existing licensable activities under the relevant existing licence or, if there is more than one relevant existing licence, the relevant existing licences.

(6) Subject to sections 19, 20 and 21 and the remaining provisions of this paragraph, the new licence must be granted subject to such conditions as reproduce the effect of—

(a) the conditions subject to which the relevant existing licence has effect at the time the application is granted, or

(b) if there is more than one relevant existing licence, all the conditions subject to which those licences have effect at that time.

(7) Where the new licence authorises the supply of alcohol, the new licence must designate the person named in the application under paragraph 2(4)(b) as the premises supervisor.

(8) The new licence must also be granted subject to conditions which reproduce the effect of any restriction imposed on the use of the premises for the existing licensable activities under the relevant existing licence or licences by any enactment specified for the purposes of this Part.

(9) In determining those restrictions, the relevant licensing authority must have regard to any children's certificate which accompanied (or a certified copy of which accompanied) the application and which remains in force.

(10) Nothing in sub-paragraph (6) or (8) requires the new licence to be granted for a limited period.

(11) But, where the application under paragraph 2 includes a request for the new licence to have effect for a limited period, the new licence is to be granted subject to that condition.

Variation of new licence

7 (1) A person who makes an application under paragraph 2 may (notwithstanding that no licence has yet been granted in consequence of that application) at the same time apply—

(a) under section 37 for any licence so granted to be varied so as to specify the individual named in the application as the premises supervisor, or

(b) under section 34 for any other variation of any such licence,

and for the purposes of an application within paragraph (a) or (b) the applicant is to be treated as the holder of that licence.

(2) In relation to an application within sub-paragraph (1)(a) or (b), the relevant licensing authority may discharge its functions under section 35 or 39 only if, and when, the application under paragraph 2 has been granted.

(3) Where an application within sub-paragraph (1)(a) or (b) is not determined by the relevant licensing authority within the period of two months beginning with the day the application was received by the authority, it is to be treated as having been rejected by the authority under section 35 or 39 (as the case may be) at the end of that period.

Existing licence revoked after grant of new licence

8 (1) This paragraph applies where the relevant licensing authority grants a new licence under this Part in respect of one or more existing licences.

(2) If sub-paragraph (4) applies to the existing licence (or each of the existing licences) which the new licence succeeds, the new licence lapses.

(3) If—

(a) where the new licence relates to more than one relevant existing licence, sub-paragraph (4) applies to one or more, but not all, of those licences, or

(b) sub-paragraph (4) applies to a children's certificate in respect of the premises,

the licensing authority must amend the new licence so as to remove from it any provision which would not have been included in it but for the existence of any existing licence or certificate to which sub-paragraph (4) applies.

(4) This sub-paragraph applies to an existing licence or children's certificate if—

(a) it is revoked before the second appointed day, or

(b) where an appeal against a decision to revoke it is pending immediately before that day, the appeal is dismissed or abandoned.

(5) Any amendment under sub-paragraph (3) takes effect when it is notified to the holder of the new licence by the relevant licensing authority.

(6) The relevant licensing authority must give a copy of any notice under sub-paragraph (5) to the chief officer of police for the police area (or each police area) in which the premises to which the new licence relates are situated.

Appeals

9 (1) Where an application under paragraph 2 is rejected (in whole or in part) by the relevant licensing authority, the applicant may appeal against that decision.

(2) Where a licensing authority grants such an application (in whole or in part), any chief officer of police who gave a notice in relation to it under paragraph 3(2) or (3) (that was not withdrawn) may appeal against that decision.

(3) Where a licence is amended under paragraph 8, the holder of the licence may appeal against that decision.

(4) Section 181 and paragraph 9(1) and (2) of Schedule 5 (general provision about appeals against decisions under Part 3 of this Act) apply in relation to appeals under this paragraph as they apply in relation to appeals under Part 1 of that Schedule.

(5) Paragraph 9(3) of that Schedule applies in relation to an appeal under sub-paragraph (2).

False statements

10 (1) A person commits an offence if he knowingly or recklessly makes a false statement in or in connection with an application under paragraph 2.

(2) For the purposes of sub-paragraph (1) a person is to be treated as making a false statement if he produces, furnishes, signs or otherwise makes use of a document that contains a false statement.

(3) A person guilty of an offence under this section is liable on summary conviction to a fine not exceeding level 5 on the standard scale.

Opening hours

11 (1) This paragraph applies where—

(a) within such period (of not less than six months) as may be specified, the holder of a justices' licence for any premises applies, in accordance with Part 3 of this Act, for the grant of a premises licence in respect of those premises, and

(b) the licence, if granted in the form applied for, would authorise the sale by retail of alcohol.

(2) In determining the application for the premises licence under section 18, the relevant licensing authority may not, by virtue of subsection (3)(b) of that section, grant the licence subject to conditions which prevent the sale of alcohol on the premises during the permitted hours.

(3) But sub-paragraph (2) does not apply where—

(a) there has been a material change in circumstances since the relevant time, and

(b) the relevant representations made in respect of the application include representations made by the chief officer of police for the police area (or any police area) in which the premises are situated advocating that, for the purposes of promoting the crime prevention objective, the premises licence ought to authorise the sale of alcohol during more restricted hours than the permitted hours.

(4) In this paragraph—

"permitted hours" means the permitted hours during which the holder of the justices' licence is permitted to sell alcohol on the premises under Part 3 of the 1964 Act;

"relevant representations" has the meaning given in section 18(6); and

"relevant time" means the time when the justices' licence was granted or, if it has been renewed, the last time it was renewed.

Provisional licences

12 (1) Where—

(a) during such period as may be specified the relevant licensing authority receives an application in accordance with Part 3 of this Act for the grant of a premises licence in respect of any premises ("the relevant premises"),

(b) under section 6 of the 1964 Act, a provisional grant of a justices' licence has been made for—

(i) the relevant premises or a part of them, or

(ii) premises that are substantially the same as the relevant premises or a part of them, and

(c) the conditions of sub-paragraph (2) are satisfied,

the licensing authority must have regard to the provisional grant of the justices' licence when determining the application for the grant of the premises licence.

(2) The conditions are—

(a) that the provisional grant of the justices' licence has not been declared final, and

(b) that the premises to which the provisional grant relates have been completed in a manner which substantially complies with the plans deposited under the 1964 Act or, as the case may be, with those plans with modifications consented to under section 6(3) of that Act.

PART 2

CLUB PREMISES CERTIFICATES

Introductory

13 (1) In this Part—

"existing club certificate" means a certificate held by a club under Part 2 of the 1964 Act for any premises;

"existing qualifying club activities" means the qualifying club activities authorised by the relevant existing club certificate in respect of those premises;

"first appointed day" means such day as may be specified as the first appointed day for the purposes of this Part;

"relevant existing club certificate", in relation to an application under paragraph 14, means the existing club certificate to which the application relates;

"relevant licensing authority" has the same meaning as in Part 4 of this Act (club premises certificates); and

"second appointed day" means such day as may be specified as the second appointed day for the purposes of this Part.

(2) In the application of section 68 (relevant licensing authority in Part 4 of this Act) for the purposes of this Part, the reference in subsection (4) of that section to an applicant for a club premises certificate is to be read as a reference to an applicant under paragraph 14 for the grant of a certificate under paragraph 16.

Application for conversion of existing club certificate

14 (1) This paragraph applies where, in respect of any premises, a club holds an existing club certificate on the first appointed day.

(2) The club may, within the period of six months beginning with the first appointed day, apply to the relevant licensing authority for the grant of a certificate under paragraph 16 to succeed the existing club certificate so far as it relates to those premises.

(3) An application under this Part must specify the existing qualifying club activities and such other information as may be specified.

(4) The application must also be in the specified form and accompanied by—

(a) the relevant documents, and

(b) the specified fee.

(5) The relevant documents are—

(a) the relevant existing club certificate (or a certified copy of it),

(b) a plan in the specified form of the premises to which that certificate relates, and

(c) such other documents as may be specified.

(6) In this paragraph any reference to a certified copy of a document is a reference to a copy of that document certified to be a true copy—

(a) by the chief executive of the licensing justices for the licensing district in which the premises are situated,

(b) by a solicitor or notary, or

(c) by a person of a specified description.

(7) A document which purports to be a certified copy of an existing club certificate is to be taken to be such a copy unless the contrary is shown.

Police consultation

15 (1) Where a person makes an application under paragraph 14, he must give a copy of the application (and any documents which accompany it) to the chief officer of police for the police area (or each police area) in which the premises are situated no later than 48 hours after the application is made.

(2) Where—

(a) an appeal is pending against a decision to revoke, or to reject an application for the renewal of, the relevant existing club certificate, and

(b) a chief officer of police who has received a copy of the application under sub-paragraph (1) is satisfied that converting that existing club certificate in accordance with this Part would undermine the crime prevention objective,

he must give the relevant licensing authority and the applicant a notice to that effect.

(3) Where a chief officer of police who has received a copy of the application under sub-paragraph (1) is satisfied that, because of a material change in circumstances since the relevant time, converting the relevant existing club certificate in accordance with this Part would undermine the crime prevention objective, he must give the relevant licensing authority and the applicant a notice to that effect.

(4) For this purpose "the relevant time" means the time when the relevant existing club certificate was granted or, if it has been renewed, the last time it was renewed.

(5) The chief officer of police may not give a notice under sub-paragraph (2) or (3) after the end of the period of 28 days beginning with the day on which he received a copy of the application under sub-paragraph (1).

Determination of application

16 (1) This paragraph applies where an application is made in accordance with paragraph 14 and the applicant complies with paragraph 15(1).

(2) Subject to sub-paragraphs (3) and (5), the licensing authority must grant the application.

(3) Where a notice is given under paragraph 15(2) or (3) (and not withdrawn), the authority must—

(a) hold a hearing to consider it, unless the authority, the applicant and the chief officer of police who gave the notice agree that a hearing is unnecessary, and

(b) having regard to the notice, reject the application if it considers it necessary for the promotion of the crime prevention objective to do so.

(4) If the relevant licensing authority fails to determine the application within the period of two months beginning with the day on which it received it, then, subject to sub-paragraph (5), the application is to be treated as granted by the authority under this paragraph.

(5) An application must not be granted (and is not to be treated as granted under sub-paragraph (4)) if the existing club certificate has ceased to have effect at—

(a) the time of the determination of the application, or

(b) in a case within sub-paragraph (4), the end of the period mentioned in that sub-paragraph.

(6) Section 10 applies as if the relevant licensing authority's functions under sub-paragraph (3) were included in the list of functions in subsection (4) of that section (functions which cannot be delegated to an officer of the licensing authority).

Notification of determination and issue of new certificate

17 (1) Where an application is granted under paragraph 16, the relevant licensing authority must forthwith—

(a) give the applicant a notice to that effect, and

(b) issue the applicant with—

(i) a certificate in respect of the premises ("the new certificate") in accordance with paragraph 18, and

(ii) a summary of the new certificate.

(2) Where an application is rejected under paragraph 16, the relevant licensing authority must forthwith give the applicant a notice to that effect containing a statement of the authority's reasons for its decision to reject the application.

(3) The relevant licensing authority must give a copy of any notice it gives under sub-paragraph (1) or (2) to the chief officer of police for the police area (or each police area) in which the premises to which the notice relates are situated.

The new certificate

18 (1) The new certificate is to be treated as if it were a club premises certificate (see section 60), and sections 73, 74 and 75 apply in relation to it accordingly.

(2) The new certificate takes effect on the second appointed day.

(3) The new certificate must authorise the premises to be used for the existing qualifying club activities.

(4) Subject to sections 73, 74 and 75, the new certificate must be granted subject to such conditions as reproduce the effect of the conditions subject to which the relevant existing club certificate has effect at the time the application is granted.

(5) The new certificate must also be granted subject to conditions which reproduce the effect of any restriction imposed on the use of the premises for the existing qualifying club activities by any enactment specified for the purposes of this Part.

(6) Nothing in sub-paragraph (4) or (5) requires the new certificate to be granted for a limited period.

Variation of new certificate

19 (1) A person who makes an application under paragraph 14 may (notwithstanding that no certificate has yet been granted in consequence of that application) at the same time apply under section 84 for a variation of the certificate, and, for the purposes of such an application, the applicant is to be treated as the holder of that certificate.

(2) In relation to an application within sub-paragraph (1), the relevant licensing authority may discharge its functions under section 85 only if, and when, the application under this Part has been granted.

(3) Where an application within sub-paragraph (1) is not determined by the relevant licensing authority within the period of two months beginning with the day the application was received by the authority, it is to be treated as having been rejected by the authority under section 85 at the end of that period.

Existing club certificate revoked after grant of new certificate

20 Where the relevant licensing authority grants a new certificate under this Part, that certificate lapses if and when—

(a) the existing club certificate is revoked before the second appointed day, or

(b) where an appeal against a decision to revoke it is pending immediately before that day, the appeal is dismissed or abandoned.

Appeals

21 (1) Where an application under paragraph 14 is rejected by the relevant licensing authority, the applicant may appeal against that decision.

(2) Where a licensing authority grants such an application, any chief officer of police who gave a notice under paragraph 15(2) or (3) (that was not withdrawn) may appeal against that decision.

(3) Section 181 and paragraph 15(1) and (2) of Schedule 5 (general provision about appeals against decisions under Part 4 of this Act) apply in relation to appeals under this paragraph as they apply in relation to appeals under Part 2 of that Schedule.

(4) Paragraph 15(3) of that Schedule applies in relation to an appeal under sub-paragraph (2).

False statements

22 (1) A person commits an offence if he knowingly or recklessly makes a false statement in or in connection with an application under paragraph 14.

(2) For the purposes of sub-paragraph (1) a person is to be treated as making a false statement if he produces, furnishes, signs or otherwise makes use of a document that contains a false statement.

(3) A person guilty of an offence under this section is liable on summary conviction to a fine not exceeding level 5 on the standard scale.

PART 3

PERSONAL LICENCES

Introductory

23 (1) Paragraphs 24 to 27 apply where—

(a) during the transitional period, the holder of a justices' licence applies to the relevant licensing authority for the grant of a personal licence under section 117,

(b) the application is accompanied by the documents mentioned in sub-paragraph (3), and

(c) the applicant gives a copy of the application to the chief officer of police for the relevant licensing authority's area within 48 hours from the time the application is made.

(2) In this paragraph "transitional period" means such period (of not less than six months) as may be specified for the purposes of this Part.

(3) The documents are—

(a) the justices' licence (or a certified copy of that licence),

(b) a photograph of the applicant in the specified form which is endorsed, by a person of a specified description, with a statement verifying the likeness of the photograph to the applicant, and

(c) where the applicant has been convicted of any relevant offence or foreign offence on or after the relevant date, a statement giving details of the offence.

(4) In this paragraph any reference to a certified copy of a justices' licence is to a copy of that licence certified to be a true copy—

(a) by the chief executive of the licensing justices for the licensing district concerned,

(b) by a solicitor or notary, or

(c) by a person of a specified description.

(5) A document which purports to be a certified copy of a justices' licence is to be taken to be such a copy, unless the contrary is shown.

Section 120 disapplied

24 Section 120 (determination of application for grant) does not apply in relation to the application.

Police objections

25 (1) Sub-paragraph (2) applies where—

(a) the applicant has been convicted of any relevant offences or foreign offences on or after the relevant date, and

(b) having regard to—

(i) any conviction of the applicant for a relevant offence, and

(ii) any conviction of his for a foreign offence which the chief officer of police considers to be comparable to a relevant offence,

whether occurring before or after the relevant date, the chief officer of police is satisfied that the exceptional circumstances of the case are such that granting the application would undermine the crime prevention objective.

(2) The chief officer of police must give a notice stating the reasons why he is so satisfied (an "objection notice")—

(a) to the relevant licensing authority, and

(b) to the applicant.

(3) The objection notice must be given no later than 28 days after the day on which the chief officer of police receives a copy of the application in accordance with paragraph 23(1)(c).

(4) For the purposes of this paragraph—

(a) "relevant offence" and "foreign offence" have the meaning given in section 113, and

(b) section 114 (spent convictions) applies for the purposes of this paragraph as it applies for the purposes of section 120.

Determination of application

26 (1) The relevant licensing authority must grant the application if—

(a) it is satisfied that the applicant holds a justices' licence, and

(b) no objection notice has been given within the period mentioned in paragraph 25(3) or any notice so given has been withdrawn.

(2) Where the authority is not satisfied that the applicant holds a justices' licence, it must reject the application.

(3) Where the authority is so satisfied, but sub-paragraph (1)(b) does not apply, it—

(a) must hold a hearing to consider the objection notice, and

(b) having regard to the notice, must—

(i) reject the application if it considers it necessary for the promotion of the crime prevention objective to do so, and

(ii) grant the application in any other case.

(4) If the authority fails to determine the application within the period of three months beginning with the day on which it receives it, then, the application is to be treated as granted by the authority under this paragraph.

(5) Section 10 applies as if the relevant licensing authority's functions under sub-paragraph (3) were included in the list of functions in subsection (4) of that section (functions which cannot be delegated to an officer of the licensing authority).

(6) In the application of section 122 (notification of determinations) to a determination under this paragraph, the references to an objection notice are to be read as references to an objection notice within the meaning of paragraph 25(2).

Appeals

27 (1) Where a licensing authority rejects an application under paragraph 26, the applicant may appeal against that decision.

(2) Where a licensing authority grants an application for a personal licence under paragraph 26(3), the chief officer of police who gave the objection notice may appeal against that decision.

(3) Section 181 and paragraph 17(6) and (7) of Schedule 5 (general provision about appeals relating to personal licences) apply in relation to appeals under this paragraph as they apply in relation to appeals under paragraph 17 of that Schedule.

(4) Paragraph 17(8) of that Schedule applies in relation to an appeal under sub-paragraph (2) above.

Interpretation of Part 3

28 For the purposes of this Part—

"relevant date", in relation to the holder of a justices' licence, means—

(a) the date when the licence was granted, or

(b) where it has been renewed, the last date when it was renewed, or

(c) where it has been transferred to the holder and has not been renewed since the transfer, the date when it was transferred; and

"relevant licensing authority", in relation to an application for a personal licence under section 117, means the authority to which the application is made in accordance with that section.

PART 4

MISCELLANEOUS AND GENERAL

Consultation on licensing policy

29 Until such time as section 59 of the 1964 Act (prohibition of sale, etc. of alcohol except during permitted hours and in accordance with justices' licence etc.) ceases to have effect in accordance with this Act, section 5(3) of this Act (licensing authority's duty to consult before determining licensing policy) has effect as if for paragraphs (c) to (e) there were substituted—

"(c) such persons as the licensing authority considers to be representative of holders of existing licences (within the meaning of Part 1 of Schedule 8) in respect of premises situated in the authority's area,

(d) such persons as the licensing authority considers to be representative of clubs registered (within the meaning of the Licensing Act 1964 (c. 26)) in respect of any premises situated in the authority's area,".

Meaning of "methylated spirits" (transitory provision)

30 Until such time as an order is made under subsection (6) of section 5 of the Finance Act 1995 (c. 4) (denatured alcohol) bringing that section into force, section 191 of this Act (meaning of "alcohol") has effect as if—

(a) for subsection (1)(f) there were substituted—

"(f) methylated spirits,", and

(b) in subsection (2), the definition of "denatured alcohol" were omitted and at the appropriate place there were inserted—

"""methylated spirits" has the same meaning as in the Alcoholic Liquor Duties Act 1979 (c. 4);".

Savings

31 Notwithstanding the repeal by this Act of Schedule 12 to the London Government Act 1963 (c. 33) (licensing of public entertainment in Greater London), or of any enactment amending that Schedule, that Schedule shall continue to apply in relation to—

(a) licences granted under section 21 of the Greater London Council (General Powers) Act 1966 (c. xxviii) (licensing of public exhibitions in London), and

(b) licences granted under section 5 of the Greater London Council (General Powers) Act 1978 (c. xiii) (licensing of entertainments booking offices in London),

as it applied before that repeal.

32 (1) In Schedule 3 to the Local Government (Miscellaneous Provisions) Act 1982 (c. 30) (control of sex establishments), paragraph (ii) of the proviso to paragraph 3A (as substituted by paragraph 85(3) of Schedule 6 to this Act) does not apply in relation to a borough of a participating council (within the meaning of section 2 of the London Local Authorities Act 1990 (c. vii)) which has appointed a day under section 3 of that Act for the coming into force of section 18 of that Act (repeal of paragraph (ii) of the proviso to paragraph 3A of Schedule 3 to that Act).

(2) On or after the coming into force of paragraph 85(3) of Schedule 6 to this Act, the reference in section 18 of that Act to paragraph (ii) of the proviso to paragraph 3A of Schedule 3 to that Act is to be read as a reference to that paragraph as substituted by paragraph 85(3) of Schedule 6 to this Act.

33 Notwithstanding that by virtue of this Act the Cinemas Act 1985 (c. 13) ceases to have effect in England and Wales, section 6 of that Act (other than subsection (3)), and sections 5, 20 and 21 of that Act so far as relating to that section, shall continue to have effect there for the purposes of—

(a) paragraph 3(2)(b) of Schedule 3 to the Local Government (Miscellaneous Provisions) Act 1982 (definition of "sex cinema"), and

(b) section 3(6)(b) of the Video Recordings Act 1984 (c. 39) (exempted supplies).

Interpretation

34 In this Schedule—

"justices' licence" means a justices' licence under Part 1 of the 1964 Act;

"specified" means specified by order; and

"the 1964 Act" means the Licensing Act 1964 (c. 26).

GRANGIS - UK PUBLISHING 2022.

www.ingramcontent.com/pod-product-compliance
Lightning Source LLC
LaVergne TN
LVHW060212210926
848481LV00008B/2706